estherpress

Books for Courageous Women

ESTHER PRESS VISION

Publishing diverse voices that encourage and equip women to walk courageously in the light of God's truth for such a time as this.

BIBLICAL STATEMENT OF PURPOSE

"For if you remain silent at this time, relief and deliverance for the Jews will arise from another place, but you and your father's family will perish. And who knows but that you have come to your royal position for such a time as this?"

– Esther 4:14

What people are saying about …

Follow God's Will

"Writing with refreshing transparency, genuine empathy, and earnest sincerity, Brittany takes the reader by the hand and shows us why and how to live 'all in with God.' A delightful and very practical read!"

Gary Thomas, bestselling author, teaching
pastor at Cherry Hills Community Church

"I absolutely love Brittany's heart for helping women of all denominations both fall in love with God's Word and learn to walk it out in their day-to-day lives. If you're struggling to live out your faith the way you want to, let *Follow God's Will* inspire you to dive deeper into all that God has for you in His Word."

Amanda Pittman, founder of Confident
Woman Co., author of *Stand in Confidence*

"For the woman who wants to read her Bible and grow closer to Jesus but sometimes feels confused or frustrated … For the woman who wants to know how to follow Jesus practically and purposefully … For the woman who is looking for biblical understanding for the complicated matters of our culture … this book is for you. Brittany Ann offers encouragement that will help you weave God's Word into the fibers of your everyday life and practically apply God's Word to the situation you're facing today."

Katy McCown, author of *She Smiles without
Fear*, president of She Laughs Ministries

"At the end of the day, God's Word brings life, comfort, wisdom, and the very balm we need to our souls. Brittany Ann takes her readers on a deeper dive into the Bible, unraveling the life-altering power of its words, written thousands of years ago, and yet so relevant for the here and now. This book offers you a pathway to expand your confidence and increase your faith."

Terra A. Mattson, LMFT, LPC, executive coach, podcaster, author, cofounder of Courageous Girls and Living Wholehearted

"In *Follow God's Will*, Brittany Ann gives thoughtful and practical wisdom for anyone questioning how to live out their faith in Christ and follow God's Word. With grace and easy-to-follow, step-by-step practical guidance, Brittany gives readers the confidence to not only love God but to boldly live for Him."

Christina Patterson, president of Beloved Women

"One thing I have come to love about Brittany and her books is how she helps readers practically apply the Bible to their everyday lives. She takes complicated issues and explains how to use the Bible to come to sound convictions of faith while showing love to others. I would recommend *Follow God's Will* to anyone who has felt overwhelmed by all the rules of the Bible and missed the extravagant love God means for you to find in Him. Then share it with those around you."

Kendra Roehl, speaker, author of *One Good Word a Day, 100 Daily Acts of Friendship for Girls,* and *The One Year Daily Acts of Kindness Devotional*

"In a world full of fighting and divisiveness, *Follow God's Will* is a much-needed breath of fresh air. I love how Brittany challenges, inspires, and equips Christian women of all denominations and walks of life to dive into Scripture and learn how to hear from God for themselves. This is a much-needed tool for women today."

Melissa S. Botts, leader at 4:20 Fire
Church in Columbus, Ohio;
mentor/leader for addictions & recovery

"Through personal yet relatable stories, alongside easy to understand yet profound teaching, Brittany Ann is gifted at providing the knowledge and know-how to help you grow closer to Jesus."

Katie Orr, Bible teacher, author of *Secrets of the
Happy Soul* and the *FOCUSed15* Bible study series

Biblical Guidelines
for Everyday Life

Follow
God's
Will

Brittany Ann

ep

estherpress

Books for Courageous Women
from David C Cook

FOLLOW GOD'S WILL
Published by Esther Press,
An Imprint of David C Cook
4050 Lee Vance Drive
Colorado Springs, CO 80918 U.S.A.

Integrity Music Limited, a Division of David C Cook
Brighton, East Sussex BN1 2RE, England

Library of Congress Control Number 2022935569
ISBN 978-0-8307-8099-0
eISBN 978-0-8307-8127-0

© 2022 Equipping Godly Women Ministries, LLC

The Team: Susan McPherson, Stephanie Bennett, Judy Gillispie,
James Hershberger, Susan Murdock, Angela Messinger
Cover Design: James Hershberger
Cover Photo: Getty Images

Printed in the United States of America
First Edition 2022

1 2 3 4 5 6 7 8 9 10

062222

To my husband.
Watching you continually seek to better live out
God's will each day inspires me to do the same.
I truly admire your strong faith, your perseverance,
and your consistent pursuit of excellence.

Teach me, LORD, the meaning of Your statutes,
and I will always keep them.
Help me understand Your instruction,
and I will obey it
and follow it with all my heart.
Help me stay on the path of Your commands,
for I take pleasure in it.
Turn my heart to Your decrees
and not to material gain.
Turn my eyes
from looking at what is worthless;
give me life in Your ways....
How I long for Your precepts!
Give me life through Your righteousness.

Psalm 119:33–37, 40 (HCSB)

Contents

Introduction

"My brother finally told my parents he's gay."

"Really? How did they take it?" I set down my sandwich to give her my full attention, the busy restaurant noises quickly fading into the background.

"Not great … and I don't know what to do. I know what the Bible says, but he's my brother. I'm not going to disown him." She sighed before continuing: "I just want him to be happy. He deserves to be happy too."

I took another sip of water, unsure how to respond. Having grown up in conservative Christian families, she and I were both well aware of the church's teachings on homosexuality. And yet the familiar refrain of "love the sinner, hate the sin" suddenly felt woefully inadequate.

How could she love and support her brother while staying true to her faith? What would that look like, practically speaking? I desperately wished I had some wise advice or perspective to share with her, but even after decades in the church, I had nothing.

She had an important decision to make. I just wanted to help her make the right one.

As a Christian author and speaker, I frequently get questions like this—from my readers online at Equipping Godly Women and from friends and family I know personally.

Questions like, "I recently found out my unmarried niece is pregnant and considering abortion, and I'm not sure how to react. I firmly believe abortion is wrong, but I don't want to overstep my boundaries. Should I confront her or leave it alone?"

And, "I know the Bible says divorce is wrong, but I'm not sure how much more I can take. My husband keeps promising he'll change, but I haven't seen any progress. How long do I have to wait?"

Do you ever struggle with questions like these?

Maybe you have friends, family, or coworkers who aren't living a Christian lifestyle, and you're not sure how to respond. Maybe you have your own decisions to make, but you're not sure which path God would want you to take. Or maybe you want to better understand how some of the Bible's more difficult commands apply in our current culture.

If so, you're definitely not alone.

When I surveyed my readers at Equipping Godly Women to learn what questions they had about following God's will today, the responses came pouring in.

> "I try to read my Bible regularly, but I don't always understand what I'm reading. How can I determine what a passage means and how I'm supposed to live it out?"

"How can I figure out God's will for my life personally? And how do I know if something is actually
God's will or just my own idea (or worse, the Enemy
trying to trick me)?"

"How vocal should I be about controversial issues
like homosexuality and transgender lifestyles? Can
I state God's truth, or do I have to stay silent so I
don't offend anyone?"

"How can I share the gospel without being rude,
pushy, or judgmental?"

These are fantastic questions, and we'll look at each more in-
depth later in this book.

In my previous book, *Fall in Love with God's Word: Practical
Strategies for Busy Women,* I share encouraging tips and advice to help
Christian women enjoy consistent, meaningful time in God's Word.
This is an incredibly important, foundational first step. After all, we
can't follow God's will if we don't know what it is. And reading the
Bible is one of the best ways we can learn more about God and what
He asks of us today.

Yet simply *reading* God's Word isn't enough. We also need to
know how to *apply* the Bible's general wisdom to the specific situations and decisions we face each day.

We need to know how to discern God's will for our lives individually, and we need to find practical, doable ways to follow God's

will on an everyday basis. Unfortunately, as the examples above demonstrate, this isn't always easy or straightforward to do.

Yes, the Bible offers us a wealth of wisdom, insight, and instruction for wise living, but we may not always know how these instructions—written thousands of years ago to people who lived in entirely different cultures than our own—should apply within the context of our culture today.

The Bible doesn't explicitly address every issue we might encounter today. And even when it does address a specific topic, Scripture typically offers stories, parables, and general guidelines rather than clear, step-by-step instructions for us to follow.

As a result, it isn't uncommon for us to know *what* God wants us to do in general (love our neighbors, respect our husbands, raise our kids well …), while still being completely uncertain on *how* to follow God's will on a very practical, day-to-day basis.

This was the problem I faced during lunch with my friend, and it's the same problem so many of us Christian women face today. We want to read God's Word and follow God's will, but we don't always know what that looks like, practically speaking.

This is exactly why I wrote this book.

Here's What You Can Expect

If you're looking for easy, overly simplistic answers for the tricky situations you're currently dealing with, I'm sorry to tell you, you won't find them here. People are unique, relationships can be complicated, and advice that works well in one situation may completely backfire in another.

Instead, **my goal for this book is to teach you a biblical framework you can use to hear God's voice, understand His Word, and determine His will for your life** *for yourself.*

In part 1, we'll answer the question "What does God want me to do?"

First, we'll start broad, by looking at the general commands Jesus gives all Christians in the Gospels. Then we'll narrow in to figure out what God might be asking *you personally* to do.

I'll teach you how to use Scripture, the prompting of the Holy Spirit, and the opportunities all around you to discover God's will for your life. And I'll help you figure out if it's really God's voice you're hearing or merely your own thoughts instead.

In part 2, we'll look to Scripture to help us respond to many of the specific questions and situations Christian women commonly encounter today, including:

- How do I live out my faith on a day-to-day basis?
- How do I live out my faith when others disagree?
- How should I navigate relationships with non-Christians?
- How can I share the gospel without being weird or pushy?
- When should I confront others' sin, and how?
- How can I follow God's will faithfully when life is hard?

These are big, complicated questions, and I won't pretend to have all the answers. We're all beautifully unique, with different needs, personalities, backgrounds, and preferences. So what works well in my family may not work in yours, and vice versa.

For this reason, following God's will can't be an overly simplistic, one-size-fits-all formula that looks the exact same for everyone. Yes, there are biblical truths and tenets that never change, but the way we live out our faith day to day will naturally vary based on our unique needs, abilities, and preferences.

That's why, throughout this book, in addition to sharing my own advice and step-by-step instruction, I'm also including numerous stories and examples from a wide variety of Jesus-loving women who come from different backgrounds and denominations. Hopefully, their stories will inspire you with ideas for what following God's will might look like for *you* (even if it's a little different than the examples you read here).

But rest assured: no matter what advice we land on, it will always be firmly rooted in God's Word. In fact, you'll find multiple opportunities in each chapter to dive deeper into Scripture to see what the Bible has to say about each topic.

Complete the "Dive Deeper into Scripture" sections throughout this book, and by the time you're done, you'll be able to confidently turn to God's Word for yourself—no matter what your questions may be. (And that's a very important skill to have.)

About the *Follow God's Will* Companion Workbook

Because this book is designed to teach you a reliable, biblical process for discerning God's will for your life (rather than simply giving you all the answers), you will want to take notes, answer questions, and complete the "Dive Deeper into Scripture" short Bible study sections as you read. This will help you take the general principles you're learning and find ways to apply them to your own life individually—so you don't just get smarter but you actually experience real life change.

You're welcome to grab any pen and notebook you have on hand, but I'd highly encourage you to check out the *Follow God's Will* companion workbook as well.

Designed to walk you chapter by chapter through the material in this book, the companion workbook contains tons of additional examples, helpful exercises, insightful questions, beautiful printables, and plenty of space to write, brainstorm, and plan—all intentionally created to help you put everything you're learning into practice on a personal level.

You can find the companion workbook, along with a growing collection of free resources to help you better follow God's will, at EquippingGodlyWomen.com/follow-gods-will.

Part I

Discover God's Will

I

The Two Greatest Commandments

What does God ask of us?

After a long week of frustrating tech issues, too much work piling up, three noisy kids home on summer break, and not nearly enough sleep, one misplaced comment was all it took to set me off.

"It feels like no matter what I do or how hard I try, it's never enough," I explained angrily, trying to keep my voice just quiet enough that the kids wouldn't hear me crying ... again.

The last thing I wanted was to ruin a beautiful Saturday afternoon. But once the tears started flowing, I couldn't stop them.

My husband quickly ushered me inside, away from little ears, as I continued: "I'm trying *so hard* to work, watch the kids, keep the house clean, run the errands, pay the bills, keep the puppy from destroying absolutely everything ... I'm trying to do everything all at once. And I'm just ... *exhausted.*"

Hi. My name is Brittany, and I'm a grade-A perfectionist. I wish I could say "recovering perfectionist." That would certainly sound better. But that's not entirely accurate.

Some days, I don't feel like a perfectionist at all. I happily let my "good enough" be good enough. I give myself plenty of grace, and I refuse to beat myself up for not achieving standards that are clearly unrealistic.

Other days ... my relentless pursuit of perfection leaves me well past the point of burnout and threatens to drive me (and everyone around me) crazy.

All my closest friends and family have had conversations with me at some point about my unrealistic expectations. A few have even suggested counseling. Now they just give me looks. Their raised eyebrows and unamused expressions tell me, "You're doing it again. You need to chill."

They're probably right. I should chill. But this doesn't stop my inner voice from insisting, *It isn't enough. You're not enough. Anything less than perfect means you're a failure. More, more, more!*

Have you ever felt this way?

You don't have to consider yourself a perfectionist to struggle under the oppressive weight of "enough." If you're anything like most of the women I talk to, you feel it too.

You want *so badly* to be that amazing Christian woman, wife, mother, friend, sister, or coworker. You want a strong faith you aren't afraid to share with others and a deeply fulfilling marriage that inspires those around you. You want to follow God's unique call on your life, and you want to be a fun mom who teaches her children how to love Jesus well.

But you aren't always sure what that looks like or how to get there.

You're doing your best, but even your best never seems quite good enough.

Maybe you've tried reading Scripture for answers and advice but you struggle to connect the Bible's epic stories and lofty wisdom to your day-to-day life. You know you're supposed to love your neighbor, respect your husband, and raise your children well, but ... *how?*

Maybe you used to dream about being a missionary and making a real difference in the world—back when you were younger. But now you have a job, a mortgage, lunches to pack, and laundry to fold. You wake up, blink, and another week is gone before you know it.

So you do what you can. *Sunday morning church. Thursday night Bible study. Prayers around the dinner table. Read your Bible when you remember.*

But when you lie in bed at night, you worry: *Maybe it isn't enough. More, more, more.*

Dive Deeper into Scripture

Be sure to grab your Follow God's Will *companion workbook (or a notebook and pen) so you can answer the questions in this book as you go. They will really help you understand and apply everything you're learning!*

→ Read Matthew 11:28–30. What does this passage tell you about God's wishes and expectations for you? How does this compare with your expectations for yourself?

→ Read 2 Corinthians 12:7b–10. What obstacle does Paul
  face in this passage? Who gave him this obstacle, and
  why? (Look carefully!) How does Paul feel about this
  obstacle by the end of the passage?

Spiritual Overachievers

If anyone knew how to push themselves to achieve more, more,
more, it was the Pharisees—a group of influential religious leaders
who often clashed with Jesus during His time on earth.

These spiritual overachievers didn't merely follow the more
than six hundred Old Testament laws God had given their ancestors generations before.[1] They committed their lives to studying the
Scriptures, finding new ways to obey God's commands more fully,
and teaching others to do the same.

One way they did this was through the creation of the Mishnah,
an oral commentary that explained and expanded on Old Testament
law by providing additional rules and guidelines.[2]

While the original intent of the Mishnah was simply to help the
Israelite people better understand how to live out God's law—which
would have been helpful—it quickly became a heavy burden, both
for the Pharisees and for everyone around them.

According to author Jerry Bridges, the Pharisees created
"hundreds of elaborate but petty rules that they had devised for
interpreting the law of God. Not only did they devise these hundreds
of man-made rules, but they had also elevated them to the level of
Scripture, so that to break one of their rules was to violate the law of
God itself."[3]

Surely God would have been pleased with these spiritual over-achievers, who worked *so hard* to keep every letter of the law and then some, right?

And yet, we see Jesus publicly rebuke the Pharisees for this exact behavior in Matthew 23:4, 23–26, when He says:

> [The Pharisees] tie up heavy, cumbersome loads and put them on other people's shoulders, but they themselves are not willing to lift a finger to move them....
>
> Woe to you, teachers of the law and Pharisees, you hypocrites! You give a tenth of your spices—mint, dill and cumin. But you have neglected the more important matters of the law—justice, mercy and faithfulness. You should have practiced the latter, without neglecting the former. You blind guides! You strain out a gnat but swallow a camel.
>
> Woe to you, teachers of the law and Pharisees, you hypocrites! You clean the outside of the cup and dish, but inside they are full of greed and self-indulgence. Blind Pharisee! First clean the inside of the cup and dish, and then the outside also will be clean.

While their devotion to God's law was certainly admirable, the Pharisees completely missed the point. They chose rules over relationship, and they and their followers paid the price. They missed out on a close relationship with the Savior of the world because they were more concerned with knowing God's commands than knowing God Himself.

Unfortunately, despite the many warnings in Scripture, many churches, religious leaders, and individual Christians fall into this same trap. In their attempts to help people avoid sin, many hand out new rules and regulations left and right.

In fact, it seems as though every time I log on to social media, I'm bombarded with new (and often contradictory) expectations for what "good Christians" should and shouldn't do.

According to some, "good Christians" don't support businesses like Target, Amazon, Starbucks, Walmart, Nike, Girl Scouts, Home Depot, or Disney. "Good Christians" don't vote for political candidates who support abortion, fund the rich, fund the poor, refuse to help those in need, or bully those who don't look or sound like them.

According to others, "good Christians" don't pursue wealth, don't get into debt, don't go on lavish vacations, and don't accept handouts. "Good Christians" don't question authority, don't stay silent in the face of injustice, don't ever miss church, and don't wear tank tops, yoga pants, pajamas, jeans, or bikinis in public.

The list goes on and on (and frequently contradicts itself).

Now, to be clear, there's nothing wrong with setting reasonable rules and guidelines for ourselves, our families, and our church members. The Old Testament makes it clear that God does have rules and guidelines He expects us to follow, just as we have many important rules and guidelines for our society and our relationships as well.

(Can you imagine a society without *any* laws? Or a marriage relationship where *any* type of behavior is acceptable? No, thank you!)

The problem happens when we become so focused on following these rules (whether God-given or man-made) that we completely forget the purpose they were intended to serve in the first place.

When we turn Christianity into little more than a checklist of dos and don'ts (or worse, a way of determining who is "in" or "out"), rather than a relationship with the God who loves us ...

When we get so caught up in being on the right side of the latest political or social justice debate that we wind up fighting people instead of problems ...

When we spend more time slandering our opponents than seeking solutions—all while the world watches and takes note ...

These are easy traps to fall into.

Thankfully, Jesus shows us a better way.

Dive Deeper into Scripture

→ Read Matthew 23:1–7, 23, 27–28. How would you describe Jesus' attitude toward the Pharisees? What specific behavior was Jesus reacting to? What did He want the Pharisees to do instead?

→ Read I Samuel 13:11–14; 16:1, 6–13. Why did God remove Saul as king over Israel? What quality did God look for in Israel's future king? What qualities do you think God looks for in His followers today?

The Two Greatest Commandments

Several months ago, I asked my husband what his perfect day would look like if he could choose anything at all. He described a fun day of fishing with the kids, frying up the fish he caught for dinner, and spending quality time together as a family until bedtime. It sounded very relaxing.

When it was my turn, I already had my perfect day all planned.

"I would wake up around six and spend an hour or two reading and studying Scripture. Then I'd go for a five- or six-mile run before it gets too hot—" I began.

"Wait, what about breakfast?" he interrupted.

"I'm getting there. After my run, I'd shower, eat breakfast, and take my time getting ready. Then I'd go to the library to write for five or six hours before taking a break to meet you for an early lunch around eleven thirty.

"After lunch, I'd work from home for another four or five hours before picking the kids up from school. The kids and I would run errands, clean the house, and play before I'd take a break to cook a delicious, healthy dinner from scratch. (The kids would all rave about my cooking, of course.)

"Everyone would help clean up after dinner, and then we'd play board games, go on a bike ride, and play baseball at the park for a few hours until bedtime at eight."

By this point, my husband looked very confused. "Your math isn't adding up …"

"I know. But this is my perfect day, and I need a lot of hours to fit it all in!"

Do you ever feel like you have too much to do and not nearly enough time to do it in? I feel this way constantly.

I want to do *all the things*, but no matter how hard I try, I can't find a way to squeeze thirty-six hours of activities into my twenty-four-hour day.

This is why we're not nearly as involved in church as I'd like to be, I don't currently volunteer anywhere (even though I really want to), and I rarely play Legos or do fun crafts with my littles, even though I know they'd love that.

I feel sad, guilty, and disappointed about every single one of these things. But there are only so many hours in a day and only so much of me to go around! (Can you relate?)

Apparently, some of the Pharisees felt this same pinch as well.

In Matthew 22:36, we see an expert of the Law ask Jesus an interesting question: "Teacher, which is the greatest commandment in the Law?"

It makes sense that he would ask this. Following every letter of the Law (and the Mishnah) would have been exhausting, if not impossible. Many didn't feel up to the task, and most Jews didn't even try.[4]

In fact, rather than attempting to follow *all* the laws, some influential Pharisees chose to go the opposite direction. They taught that the Jewish people didn't have to follow the entire Law—only the rules the Pharisees felt were most important.[5]

Now, this particular Pharisee wanted Jesus' opinion on the matter. Would Jesus affirm the Pharisees' strict rule-following ways, stating that even the most obscure commandment must be followed to the letter? Or would Jesus ease the Jewish people's burden by highlighting one particular type of command the people could focus on, without worrying about the rest? What did the people actually need to do to please God, and what could they safely neglect?

Chances are, you're familiar with Jesus' reply in verses 37–40:

> Jesus replied: "'Love the Lord your God with all
> your heart and with all your soul and with all your
> mind.' This is the first and greatest commandment.
> And the second is like it: 'Love your neighbor as
> yourself.' All the Law and the Prophets hang on
> these two commandments."

Don't miss the significance of this passage. Here, Jesus isn't giving the Pharisees another rule to add to their long list of rules to follow. He's saying, This is the main idea! If you get *nothing* else from everything I've taught, don't miss this.

Every single command in all of Scripture is ultimately meant to help us do one of two things: love God and love others. It all points back to this.

Dive Deeper into Scripture

→ Read Matthew 22:37–40. How do these two commandments fit into the rest of the law? What might this mean for us today, practically speaking?

→ Read Deuteronomy 6:1–3. Why did God give the Israelites the Old Testament laws? (Hint: Look for the repeated phrase "so that.")

→ Read Romans 13:8–10. Why do you think Paul uses the phrase "continuing debt" in verse 8? How is love the fulfillment of the law (v. 10)?

What Love Is … and Is Not

A few nights ago, my husband made an observation that struck me as odd: "I'm not as romantic as I used to be—"

"What are you talking about?" I quickly interrupted. "Just this morning you made me a fancy latte, you took an hour off work to spend time with me, you took the kids outside to play during my work meeting this afternoon, you spent the last hour grilling a delicious steak to share, *and* you cleaned up the kitchen without being asked. And that's just today—a completely normal, average Tuesday." (I'm spoiled. I know.)

Sure, my husband doesn't buy me flowers and jewelry as often as he did when we were dating, but that's because he knows I don't *want* him to.

To me, *love* doesn't mean extravagant gifts, expensive jewelry, fancy vacations, or even a bouquet of roses now and then. I'd much rather have the simple, everyday gestures that say, "I see you, I care about you, and your thoughts and feelings matter to me."

Depending on where you look or who you ask, our society offers several different (and often contradictory) ideas of what love should look like.

For example, love is often described as:

- accepting others exactly as they are, without noticing or mentioning their faults
- bluntly pointing out others' sins and shortcomings so they can improve (and not lead others astray)

- boldly standing up for victims of oppression and injustice (including yourself)
- allowing others to repeatedly treat you poorly while you "turn the other cheek"
- insisting that others look, think, feel, or believe exactly as you do (because you know what's best for them)
- being nice and agreeable to everyone, so as not to cause others to feel uncomfortable or make waves

As Christians, we believe that Jesus offers us the perfect example of pure, selfless love. But when we study how Jesus treated those around Him in the Gospels, His behavior doesn't always fit neatly into any one of these descriptions.

Jesus wasn't always "nice." He told the truth boldly, He offended people regularly, and He wasn't afraid to flip tables when needed.[6] His words were sometimes blunt and shocking, but He wasn't interested in forcing others to conform to His beliefs, and He certainly wasn't cruel. He was the first to forgive, saw the best in people, and had no problem associating with social outcasts and "sinners," even when it affected His reputation.[7]

Unfortunately, Scripture never shares an exact definition or step-by-step guide to loving our neighbors.

Instead, from the Old Testament provisions for widows to the parable of the good Samaritan to Jesus' own death on the cross, we're given plenty of general commands, stories, parables, and examples to follow. It's up to us to extract meaning from these passages and then find ways to apply their lessons to our own lives. (I'll share how to do this in chapter 3.)

To me, **loving others means respecting the inherent worth and dignity of each person as a human being made in the image of God, and proactively finding ways to treat others the way you would want to be treated** (adjusting for personality differences and personal preference, of course).

This definition reminds me that we're all human. We all sin, fall short, and make mistakes. We're *all* still a work in progress, and we all need plenty of grace for the journey. Your struggle isn't necessarily my struggle, but we all struggle with something.

And we're all human beings, made in the image of God. We *all* deserve respect, dignity, and love—not because of what we've accomplished, what title we hold, what we look like, or who we are, but because of *whose* we are. We're all princes and princesses, children of the King (even if we don't always act like it).

As a mama, I would *never* want to see another person bullying or harassing one of my children—even if my child had done something to start the fight, whether intentionally or unintentionally. And I'm confident God feels the same way about His children as well.

How often do we forget this?

You know that politician you're convinced is out to destroy Christianity as we know it? *He's a human being, made by God, with inherent worth and dignity.*

The difficult and dismissive customer service representative you spoke with on the phone last week? *She's a human being, made by God, with inherent worth and dignity.*

The homeless person you pretend not to notice on your morning commute? *He's a human being, made by God, with inherent worth and dignity.*

The group of people supporting the cause you vehemently disagree with? *They're human beings, made by God, with inherent worth and dignity.*

Your stubborn husband, meddling mother-in-law, obnoxious neighbor, annoying coworker, and the reckless driver who cut you off in traffic this morning? *They're all human beings, made by God, with inherent worth and dignity, and they deserve to be treated as such.*

Sadly, it's incredibly common to see self-proclaimed Christians bickering and name-calling over each new hot-button issue—all while the world watches and takes note.

Abortion ... LGBTQ rights ... immigration laws ... racial justice ... gender inequality ... health care mandates ... political platforms ...

These are all incredibly important issues, and we all have a responsibility to do what we can to step up and make the world a better place.

Yet, in our zeal to uphold our religious beliefs, have we forgotten what it means to be a Christ follower, first and foremost? (Remember those Pharisees who were so obsessed with following the rules that they missed the whole point?)

Have we become so preoccupied with making sure everyone follows *our* ideas, *our* rules, and *our* interpretation of Scripture that we've completely lost sight of what Jesus tells us are the two most important commands of all—to love God and others?

What would it look like if we, as Christians, were willing to assume the same posture of humility and service that Jesus demonstrated in the Bible? What if, rather than bickering over which behaviors are right or wrong, godly or ungodly, we simply stopped and looked for ways to love the people right in front of us well?

What if, instead of arguing about politics with strangers on social media, we committed to pray for our nation's leaders to have the wisdom, courage, and conviction to lead our country well?

What if, instead of complaining about state abortion laws, we committed to mentor at-risk teens, donate to crisis pregnancy centers, or provide affordable childcare for women in need?

What if we joined school boards, ran for government offices, voted in local elections, started good businesses, or donated our time, money, or knowledge to various nonprofits in our community?

What if we mentored young wives, coordinated meals for grieving church members, checked in on our elderly neighbors, had real conversations with nonbelievers, or took the time to find out how our friends and family are *really* doing these days?

This, my friend, is the point of the gospel.

Not that we collect enough spiritual accolades to make God proud, that we memorize enough random Bible facts to impress our friends, that we consistently defend our beliefs against those who disagree, that we always say or do the right thing in every situation, or even that our beliefs are always 100 percent correct on every minor issue.

Christianity, at its very core, is about loving God and loving others well.

If we miss this one crucial truth, we've missed the whole point.

2

The Four Calls on Every Christian's Life

What does Jesus want us to do?

I've been known to give my children some pretty strange rules from time to time. Rules such as "Don't hide a wild elephant under your bed and feed him Cheetos" and "Don't run through the grocery store naked, screaming 'Spaghetti, spaghetti, spaghetti!' at the top of your lungs." (The more outlandish, the better!)

My kids are still young enough to find this hilarious. And I find it's a fun way to make an important point: that I shouldn't have to spell out every single behavior my children should or shouldn't do. Some rules should go without saying.

When my children were toddlers, it made sense to give them specific instructions and constant redirections. They were still learning right from wrong, discovering cause and effect, and developing self-control. That's understandable.

Now that they're all in elementary and middle school, however, they don't need me to spell everything out for them. They're old enough and smart enough to figure some things out on their own—based on their experience and the guidance I've given them so far—and I often expect them to do so.

Sometimes I'll give one general reminder, such as "Behave yourselves," if it's pretty obvious what they should or shouldn't be doing. But "Behave yourselves" can leave a lot of room for interpretation. (For example, Does pelting each other with Nerf gun darts while Mom is on an important phone call count as "behaving" as long as no one is crying … yet?)

So other times, I'll offer them a few more specific guidelines. Something super sweet and eloquent, like "I need to make an important phone call. I don't care what you do as long as you (1) don't make a mess, (2) don't pester each other, and (3) stay relatively quiet" (which, in our house, usually translates into "Yes, you may play video games").

When I simply offer a few general guidelines, my kids have a much better idea of which types of behavior I expect without my having to outline every single behavior that would or would not be okay.

Not only does this save me a ton of time and headache, but it also encourages my children to learn to make wise decisions *for themselves*—a skill they'll need to have someday when I'm not around.

As we read through the Bible, we see God follow a similar pattern with the Israelites. In the Old Testament, particularly in the books of Exodus, Leviticus, and Deuteronomy, God gives His people *incredibly* detailed instructions for resolving interpersonal conflicts, building and carrying the tabernacle, offering a variety of sacrifices, and interacting with the surrounding nations.

These detailed instructions would have been very helpful for a new nation that truly didn't know what God expected and that would have been tempted to absorb the behaviors of the surrounding pagan nations. Israel's future judges and kings also would have appreciated clear directions to help them lead the people well.

Once we reach the New Testament, however, Jesus seems far less interested in laying out a detailed list of specific rules and regulations for the people to follow.

As we saw in the previous chapter, the Pharisees already had a detailed list of rules and guidelines, and they'd gotten so caught up in trying to follow every individual rule perfectly that they largely forgot why they were following the rules in the first place. They completely missed the point!

So, in the New Testament, rather than handing out a comprehensive list of individual rules and regulations, Jesus gives His people four general commands to follow.

In addition to asking us to love God and love others (as we explored in the previous chapter), Jesus specifically calls His followers to:

1. Repent.
2. Believe in Him.
3. Follow Him.
4. Make disciples.

Let's look at each of these more in-depth.

Dive Deeper into Scripture

→ Read Romans 7:7–12. Why did God give the Israelite people a detailed set of laws if He knew they weren't going to be able to keep them? What was the intended effect of these laws (v. 7)?

→ Read John 16:12–13. According to this passage, why didn't Jesus give us a detailed list of everything we will need to know and do right? How can we receive the wisdom we need today, now that Jesus is no longer physically on earth?

I. Jesus Calls His Followers to Repent

While repentance may not be a popular sermon topic today, there's no question it was a foundational requirement during Jesus' ministry two thousand years ago.

In fact, the very first command Jesus makes in all of Scripture is a call to repentance. We see this in Matthew 4:17, which states, "From that time on Jesus began to preach, 'Repent, for the kingdom of heaven has come near.'"[1]

So what is repentance exactly, and how can we know if we've adequately repented?

Merriam-Webster defines the word *repent* this way: "to turn from sin and dedicate oneself to the amendment of one's life."[2] Far more than simply admitting your sin or feeling sorry for what you've done, true biblical repentance also requires a deliberate change in action.

Think of repentance as doing a 180. Previously, you were headed in one direction. When you repent, you stop and instead turn and head a completely different way. This applies to sin as well as false beliefs, negative thought patterns, and any other actions or behaviors that are at odds with God's will for your life.

Of course, repentance isn't always easy. After thousands of years of observation and practice, Satan is an expert at making sin look, sound, and feel appealing—at least initially.

Satan convinces us that small sins are "no big deal." Then he uses these small sins as leverage to gain even more impact and influence in our lives—often taking us where we never intended to go.

This is why it isn't enough to simply sprinkle a few good deeds onto a life that's otherwise full of sin and selfishness. Sin is like an untreated infection: allow even a little bit, and it's likely to spread.

Jesus asks us to repent so we can make room for the full and abundant life God has for us instead.

Dive Deeper into Scripture

→ Read Revelation 2:5; Acts 17:30–31; and Proverbs 28:13. Why is it important that we identify and repent of our sins, false beliefs, and negative thought patterns now, rather than waiting until later (or not repenting at all)?

→ Read 1 John 1:8–9. How does God respond when we repent? (Notice both actions.)

2. Jesus Calls His Followers to Believe in Him

The gospel of Mark describes the beginning of Jesus' ministry in a similar way as Matthew, but with additional detail and an added command.

Mark 1:14–15 tells us, "After John was put in prison, Jesus went into Galilee, proclaiming the good news of God. 'The time has come,' he said. 'The kingdom of God has come near. Repent *and believe the good news!*'"

Whether phrased as "believe" or "have faith," Jesus' second command is a recurring theme throughout the Gospels. Rather than presenting it as a new command, however, Jesus simply expects His followers to have faith in Him and is exasperated, saddened, or disappointed (depending on how you read His words) when they don't.

For example, Jesus expected Peter to have enough faith to walk on water. Matthew 14:31 tells us, "Immediately Jesus reached out his hand and caught him. 'You of little faith,' he said, 'why did you doubt?'" And after Jesus calmed the storm for His terrified disciples, He said to them, "Why are you so afraid? Do you still have no faith?" (Mark 4:40).

Not only does Jesus expect that His followers will have faith in Him, but many of Jesus' miracles were dependent on it. The Bible tells us Jesus healed a servant,[3] a bleeding woman,[4] and a Gentile girl[5] in direct response to someone's faith, but "he did not do many miracles [in his hometown] *because of their lack of faith*" (Matt. 13:58).

It's important to note, however, that in this context *believe* doesn't merely mean "believe that Jesus existed or had power." The people could clearly see He did. The Pharisees believed Jesus existed, yet they hardly believed *in* Him. (They had Him killed!)

And there are plenty of atheist and agnostic historians who will readily admit that a man named Jesus walked the earth two thousand years ago, though they don't believe He was God.

Simply believing that Jesus existed or that He was a good moral teacher isn't enough. **Jesus isn't calling us to believe that He existed but to believe that He is who He says He is and He can do what He says He can do.**

To give an analogy, think of the last time you poured yourself a glass of water. Did you carefully inspect the glass for holes or cracks before you filled it? Did you only pour a few drops at first to see if the glass would hold? After you poured the water, did you repeatedly check for signs of a leak? Did you have another glass on hand, just in case?

Chances are, you didn't do any of these things. You likely filled your glass quickly, without even thinking about it. You believed the glass would hold, and you acted according to your beliefs.

Yet **how many times do we *say* we have faith or believe in God, only for our actions to prove otherwise?**

When God asks you to do something, do you tend to procrastinate, look for a way out, or come up with excuses why you can't fully obey? Do you only partially obey until God proves Himself to you? Do you set up safeguards *just in case*? Do you constantly worry and double-check, ready to abandon ship if anything goes wrong?

Now, to be clear, I am not advocating blind faith. I firmly believe God gave us brains because He expects us to use them to think, reason, ask questions, and make wise decisions.

However, there comes a point when our human reasoning isn't enough. When we have to decide, *Do I truly believe Jesus is who He says He is and He can do what He says He can do? What do my actions say about what I truly believe?*

Dive Deeper into Scripture

→ Read Hebrews 11:1–4, 7–11, 17–34. How does the Bible define faith? How did each of these men and women demonstrate faith?

→ Read Hebrews 11:6 and Ephesians 2:8–9; 6:16. Why is faith so important, according to these passages?

3. Jesus Calls People to Follow Him

Once we've repented of our sins and chosen to walk in faith, Jesus' third command provides the logical next step: we must learn to live and love the way He did.

We see this in the Bible when Jesus calls His disciples with the phrase "Follow me."

Matthew 4:18–20 tells us, "As Jesus was walking beside the Sea of Galilee, he saw two brothers, Simon called Peter and his brother Andrew. They were casting a net into the lake, for they were fishermen. 'Come, follow me,' Jesus said, 'and I will send you out to fish for people.' At once they left their nets and followed him."

In order to understand the fullness of what Jesus was asking of these men, it's helpful to know a little background on Jewish rabbis during Jesus' time.

Jesus lived in a time and place where the men knew Scripture well, respected it highly, and debated it regularly.[6]

Young Jewish boys received an education "focused primarily on the Torah, emphasizing both reading and writing Scripture. Large portions were memorized and it is likely that many students knew the entire Torah by memory by the time this level of education was finished."[7]

While the majority of students would eventually stay home to help their families or learn trades, the most remarkable of students would continue their education by studying the Prophets and the Writings and by learning how to understand and apply Scripture for themselves.

Then a select few of the very best and brightest students could apply to study under a rabbi as one of his disciples. This was a rare and great honor reserved only for the religious elite.

You see, a rabbi's reputation rested on the quality of his followers, so rabbis were very picky about which disciples they would accept. Not only would rabbis require their disciples to meet certain qualifications and complete an application process, but "if a rabbi ultimately agreed to a would-be-disciple's request, and allowed him to become a disciple, the disciple-to-be agreed to *totally submit* to the rabbi's authority in all areas of interpreting the Scriptures for his life."[8]

Rabbis didn't teach their disciples in a once-a-week, classroom-type setting. Rather, once a disciple was accepted into a rabbi's talmidim, the rabbi and his disciples would live in close community for a period of time so the disciples could learn to emulate their rabbi.

This was an incredibly hands-on process, where the rabbi would personally invest in the small group of men, watching them live out their lives and helping to guide their thoughts and actions.

This process typically involved regularly debating the meaning and application of Scripture. Rather than handing out quick tips, easy answers, or straightforward advice, however, a rabbi would encourage and invite his disciples to think and discern for themselves. This way, the disciples would be able to live and make decisions the way their rabbi did, even after he was no longer around.

If a rabbi *did* provide an authoritative answer to settle a debate, however, all further discussion on the topic would cease. As soon as the rabbi's disciples were given a clear answer, they were expected to follow it without further debate for the rest of their lives, even after they had parted ways with the rabbi.

As a Jewish rabbi, Jesus followed a very similar process with His disciples—except, instead of waiting for the most prestigious to apply, Jesus proactively sought out a ragtag bunch no one would ever expect. Jesus didn't form an exclusive clique with the religious elite; He invited everyday, average people to follow Him and become His disciples.

And Jesus still invites each of us to follow Him today.

When Jesus says "Follow me," He isn't inviting us to evaluate His teachings so we can pick and choose which advice or guidelines we feel like following, when it's convenient for us.

He's inviting us to go on an intimate journey and an exciting adventure with Him—to discover how He lived, loved, thought, and taught, so we can do the same. He's inviting us to sit under His leadership and submit to His authority in all things.

It's a great honor but also a great responsibility.

Dive Deeper into Scripture

→ Read Matthew 4:18–22. Why do you think these men followed Jesus immediately? What might they have had to leave behind to do so?

→ Read Matthew 9:35–38. Do you think Jesus' words "The harvest is plentiful but the workers are few" still apply? Given all the miracles Jesus was performing then, why wouldn't more people have wanted to be His disciples? Why don't more people want to be His disciples today?

4. Jesus Calls His Followers to Make Disciples

On September 11, 2001, Brian David Sweeney called and left a voice mail for his wife. You may have heard it.

> Jules, this is Brian. Listen, I'm on an airplane that's been hijacked. If things don't go well, and it's not looking good, I just want you to know I absolutely love you. I want you to do good; go have a good time. Same to my parents and everybody. And I just totally love you. And I'll see you when you get there. Bye, babe. I hope I call you.[9]

Most people don't have the opportunity for last words. It's rare to know with certainty when it's our time to go. But if you knew you only had a very short amount of time left to live, you would probably want to make your words count.

This is what many people did when two planes crashed into the World Trade Center on 9/11, and it's what Jesus did when He knew His time on earth was drawing to a close.

In Matthew 28:18b–20, we read some of Jesus' final words before His ascent into heaven. Known as the Great Commission, this passage reads:

> All authority in heaven and on earth has been given to me. Therefore go and make disciples of all nations, baptizing them in the name of the Father and of the Son and of the Holy Spirit, and teaching them to obey everything I have commanded you. And surely I am with you always, to the very end of the age.

This fourth and final call (to make disciples) was a common rabbinical practice in Jesus' day. When a rabbi believed his disciples were ready, he would send them out to create disciples of their own. "He was saying 'As far as is possible you are like me. Now go and seek others who will imitate you. Because you are like me, when they imitate you they will be like me.'"[10]

Being both fully human and fully divine, Jesus could have chosen to personally appear to each of His followers throughout time, answering all their questions and teaching them everything they needed to know. But this isn't what Jesus chose to do. Jesus commissioned His disciples to make disciples who would make disciples, until the whole world hears the gospel message.

It's easy to feel like the responsibility to share the gospel is reserved for "professional Christians"—pastors, priests, missionaries, Christian authors, speakers, bloggers, and teachers. You might be tempted to think that if you don't work in a Christian profession, you're off the hook for sharing your faith.

But sharing the gospel was never meant for the select few.

Yes, Christian leaders have an important role to fulfill, but so do you. Your pastor doesn't see your neighbors, your coworkers, and your children every day. He can't possibly reach everyone on his own—which is why God is sending you!

What if God put you right where He did to reach the people you see every day—people who may never know Christ's saving power if you aren't brave enough to share it with them?

Who do you know who needs to hear the life-saving power of the gospel today?

Dive Deeper into Scripture

→ Read Acts 1:6–8. What did Jesus tell His followers they would do? What were they given (v. 8), and why?

→ Read Romans 10:14–15. Why is it so important that we share our faith with others?

What Is God's Will for Me Personally?

So far in this book, we've looked at God's general purpose for all mankind.

In chapter 1, we started broad, with what Jesus says are the two most important commands of all: to love God and love others. In this chapter, we examined the four main ways Jesus calls us to do this: by repenting, believing in Him, following Him, and making disciples.

Concerning all six of these calls, Jesus offers an *invitation* to nonbelievers (He is not demanding), but He expects His followers to still do these things today. They are required for Christ followers.

Now that we've laid this foundation, we're ready to make it practical. We want to see—in addition to what God is calling everyone to do generally—how God may be calling you to follow Him specifically.

Over the next three chapters, we'll look at three methods to help you figure out how God may be calling you to follow Him with your life—by understanding His written Word (the Bible), by hearing His spoken word (through the Holy Spirit), and by paying attention to the opportunities all around you.

Let's head there now.

3

Understanding God's Written Word

How do I apply the Bible's instructions to my life today?

When my son was four, he had a noticeable speech impediment, though I didn't realize it at the time. I knew he consistently pronounced words incorrectly, but—not being around other children his age—I thought it was normal and no big deal.

After all, *I* always knew exactly what he was saying.

I knew "pot pies" meant "french fries." (He pronounced his *f*s as *p*s.) "Ya you" meant "love you," "go ami" meant he wanted to play downstairs, and "ti tu" meant "thank you" (although it could also be used for "please").

While I could easily understand him, no one outside our immediate family could. Whenever he tried to speak to other adults, they always needed me to interpret. My son was speaking English, but the message he was trying to communicate was often lost on anyone who wasn't around him regularly.

Unfortunately, something similar can happen when we read God's Word.

Yes, our personal copies of the Bible may be written in plain English, but they're also compiled translations of original texts written thousands of years ago in cultures and languages very different than our own.

Not every word of the Bible's original manuscripts translates perfectly into our modern language, and we don't always know or understand all the unwritten nuance, implied meaning, context, and background information that would have been obvious to the Bible's original audiences.

As a result, it's easy to miss or misunderstand the message the original authors or speakers were trying to convey, especially when we're reading the Bible on our own.

This isn't to say that we can't understand Scripture on our own. We can, and the Holy Spirit empowers us to do so.[1] But **unfortunately, determining how to understand and obey the Bible's commands today isn't always as simple or straightforward as we'd like it to be.**

As a first-century Jewish rabbi, Jesus was often intentionally vague, using parables and illustrations rather than providing step-by-step instructions with clear answers, in order to teach His disciples discernment. There are many issues He never specifically addressed. And of the ones He did, His answers, as recorded in Scripture, often leave a great deal of room for interpretation.

Because of this, it's common for Christians of all backgrounds to disagree over both the meaning and the application of verses that seem like they should be clear.

I've certainly seen this in my own life. After being raised in Protestant, evangelical culture for my first twenty-plus years, I found attending Catholic mass with my husband and his family for the last eight to be a bit of a culture shock.

It isn't merely issues of theology and doctrine that differ either. Every Christian denomination emphasizes different parts of the same gospel message, and each one has its own culture, traditions, and preferences.

And even within the same faith tradition, it's incredibly common for intelligent, devoted Christians to vehemently disagree on which issues are most important or how we should live them out in our daily lives.

As committed, Jesus-loving Christians, we truly *want* to understand and obey God's Word—but the question is, *How?* How can we know *which* truths the Bible's original authors and speakers wanted to communicate? How do those truths apply in our modern culture today?

These aren't easy questions to answer, but that doesn't mean we shouldn't try. After all, Scripture is one of the primary ways God still speaks, and we don't want to miss out on what He's saying.

Dive Deeper into Scripture

→ Read Acts 20:32; 2 Timothy 3:16–17; and Hebrews 4:12. How can the Bible help us? List five specific examples.

→ Read Isaiah 55:6–7. What does this passage invite us to do? What does God promise us in return?

A Seven-Step Process for Understanding God's Word

Over the course of the next three chapters, we're going to examine three primary ways God still leads and guides us today: through His written Word (the Bible), His spoken word (the Holy Spirit), and the opportunities all around us.

Of these three, God's written Word (the Bible) is arguably the most straightforward and reliable, making it the perfect place to start. **No matter how else God may choose to guide you throughout your life, He will never contradict what He has already revealed in Scripture.**

It's up to us, of course, to know what that is.

In this chapter, I'm sharing a seven-step process you can use to help you better understand God's Word and how it applies to your life today.[2]

This process is very hands on, so you will want to take notes. Please grab a pen and notebook or the *Follow God's Will* companion workbook, if you have it. We'll work through several exercises together here. And you can find additional tips, examples, and questions in the workbook if you'd like to dive even deeper and find new ways to apply everything you're learning.

Once you have your materials ready, let's go ahead and get started.

I. Choose a Bible Passage to Study

The first step in understanding God's Word is selecting a passage to study.

If you already read your Bible regularly, this could be your daily reading.

Alternately, you may want to look up a verse or passage on a specific topic that matters to you. (For example, "What does the Bible say about [divorce, grief, worry, etc.]?") If you have a study Bible, the concordance in the back should have plenty of ideas to choose from.

Both are great options, and I often do a mix of both.

2. Pray for Guidance and Clarity

While we'll discuss the guidance of the Holy Spirit more in the next chapter, it's important to mention the power and importance of prayer here as well.

You see, the Bible isn't a static history book full of outdated information that's no longer relevant. Not only did God divinely inspire the Bible's more than sixty original authors to record His message back then,[3] but God still speaks and works in our lives through His Word even now.

Paul writes in 1 Thessalonians 2:13, "And we also thank God continually because, when you received the word of God, which you heard from us, you accepted it not as a human word, but as it actually is, *the word of God, which is indeed at work in you who believe*."

Furthermore, 2 Corinthians 3:14 tells us, "But [the Israelites'] minds were made dull, for to this day the same veil [that prevents them from fully understanding Scripture] remains when the old covenant is read. It has not been removed, because *only in Christ is it taken away*."

Yes, we can read the Bible and get some meaning from it on our own. However, to fully understand and benefit from Scripture,

we need to go beyond merely reading the words on the page to hearing God speak through the pages of His Word.

This is why it is so important to spend time in prayer before we dive into Scripture. We don't want to be satisfied by merely reading stories, poetry, and wisdom. We want to hear from God Himself. We need Him to speak to us, reveal Himself to us, and guide our understanding of the text.

Not sure what to pray? You can ask God to give you wisdom and understanding, to guide your thinking as you read the text, to reveal more of Himself and His character to you through its words, and to help you see how to apply Scripture to your life today.

These are prayers God loves to answer![4]

3. Read the Passage

After you've spent time in prayer, your next step is to read the passage to see what it says.

At this point, you aren't trying to determine what the verses mean or how they apply to your life. Instead, temporarily set aside any preconceived thoughts or ideas and simply do a straightforward, surface-level reading of the text.

Focus primarily on the nouns and verbs within the passage to answer the question, *Who does what?* Your answer should be a simple sentence or two, and it should include facts only—no opinions or application at this point.

Dive Deeper into Scripture

→ Read Mark 4:1–9. What happens in this passage?
  Write a simple one-sentence summary of the

passage, being careful not to add any additional information not found in the text.

4. Notice the Details

Once you have a broad overview of the passage you chose, your next step is to notice as many individual details as possible. Depending on the length and complexity of the reading, you might find as many as thirty or forty specific details in one passage of Scripture.

Here are a few types of details you can look for:

- nouns (names of people, places, and things)
- verbs (action words)
- adjectives (descriptive words)
- repetition (words, phrases, ideas, or concepts)
- lists (for example, the fruits of the Spirit)
- comparison and/or contrast (look for words like *and, but, while, however,* or *though*)
- cause and effect (look for words like *therefore, because,* or *for this reason*)
- conditional clauses (phrases that include *if... then*)
- questions and answers[5]

You might also ask:

- Who wrote this passage?
- Who is this passage written to or for?
- What is the genre of the passage (narrative, law, poetry, wisdom, prophecy, or epistle)?[6]

- Where is this passage found within Scripture (Old Testament, New Testament, etc.)?
- What happens immediately before or after this passage?
- What is the topic of the surrounding passages?
- What is the book about as a whole?
- What themes or patterns do I notice?

Don't worry if you can't answer all these questions right from the text. Some of this information may be found elsewhere in Scripture, in the notes provided in your study Bible, in Bible handbooks and history books, or in trusted online sources such as commentaries, sermons, or articles.

It's important to note, however: At this stage, we still aren't drawing conclusions. We're simply gathering a wealth of interesting information that may or may not be useful later.

Dive Deeper into Scripture

→ Go back to Mark 4:1–9. Make a list of at least fifteen individual details from the text, using the checklists above to help you.

5. Identify the Main Idea

I once read a story about a woman who always cut the back off her holiday ham before placing the rest in the oven. When her husband noticed this, he was curious and asked why. Why waste perfectly good holiday ham?

She replied, "It's tradition. It's the way we've always done it in our family." But now she was curious. So she asked her mother, and then her grandmother, to see if either had an explanation.

As it turns out, the woman's grandmother had started the practice. Her favorite baking pan wasn't quite big enough to hold an entire holiday ham, so she always cut the back off so the ham would fit.

Both the woman and her mother had been wasting perfectly good ham for years—all because they were still following a practice that made sense for the grandmother but which was completely unnecessary for both of them!

This brings up an important question: How many "rules" do we follow simply because they made sense for an earlier generation—not because they're the best way for us to live out our faith today?

Now, to be clear, I'm not advocating throwing biblical rules out the window. God never changes, and His values, character, and commands never change either. But sometimes the *way* we follow God's timeless commands can change, depending on the unique personalities, talents, resources, and current circumstances of those involved.

This is why, when studying Scripture, **we need to identify the main idea or core message that the author was communicating to the original audience *before* we determine how we might live out the passage today.**

This will help us avoid stubbornly holding on to outdated practices while completely missing the original purpose those practices were intended to fulfill. (Remember those Pharisees from chapter 1?)

So how do we find the main idea the Bible's original authors wanted to communicate?

According to the authors of *Grasping God's Word*, the main idea (or principle) of any biblical passage should:

- be reflected in the text
- be timeless and not tied to a specific situation
- not be culturally bound
- correspond to the teaching of the rest of Scripture
- be relevant to both the biblical and the contemporary audience[7]

If a rule or guideline that you see in Scripture doesn't meet all five of these requirements, then take a step back and think more broadly. Read the surrounding passages and research for additional information.

Ask questions such as, *Why does Scripture give us this command?* or *What did the original author or speaker ultimately want their audience to know?*

Keep reading, studying, researching, and asking questions until you find a main idea that meets all five requirements. This can take some digging, but don't skip this crucial step!

God still expects us to follow the main idea of every passage of Scripture, and we can't do that if we don't know what it is. It's the individual command (given to a specific church or individual thousands of years ago) that we may or may not have to follow exactly as written today.

Let's look at a few examples together, and you'll see what I mean.

Dive Deeper into Scripture

→ Read Deuteronomy 21:18–21. How does this passage instruct the Israelites to deal with rebellious sons and daughters? Should we deal with our rebellious children the same way today? What is the main idea of this passage? How else might we live out the main idea of this passage in our culture?

→ Read Luke 10:3–11. This passage contains several individual instructions. Which specific commands do you think we still need to follow exactly as written? What main idea(s) might we take from this passage instead?

→ Read I Timothy 5:23. Why did Paul give Timothy this command? Do we need to follow this command exactly as written? What main idea might we take from this passage instead?

6. Note Similarities and Differences between Then and Now

In light of the verses in the "Dive Deeper into Scripture" section above, we can reasonably conclude that while some biblical commands are morally binding for all believers everywhere, others were intended only for a specific individual or group at a certain point in time.

This doesn't mean that these verses aren't still helpful or inspiring for us today. But it does mean that we don't have to (and aren't supposed to) follow *every* single command in all of Scripture exactly as it was written to its original audience.

To give an example: pretend your grandfather wrote many beautiful love letters to your grandmother, which you gathered all into one collection.

Now suppose your grandfather happened to write "Don't forget to take your heart medication" in one of his letters. You wouldn't automatically assume *you* also needed to take heart medication just because your grandmother did. You would understand that particular instruction was meant for her, not for you.

You could certainly use your grandfather's loving instruction as an example. It might remind you to take good care of yourself in other ways, or it might prompt you to check in on your friends and family to see how their health has been lately. But you wouldn't follow his instruction exactly.

The main idea (take care of yourself) is helpful, but the specific application (take heart medication) was never meant for you to follow in the same manner.

Remember, there is no "letter of Paul to the church in America." Rather, the Bible is a collection of stories and letters written to specific individuals and churches at specific times and places in the past.

Yes, the Bible's wisdom, advice, and instruction can benefit all people everywhere. But this doesn't mean every command applies directly to our unique experiences today. There are some instructions we can learn and benefit from without following them exactly as written.

So how do we know *which* commands do or don't directly apply to us today?

We don't want to simply guess, following some rules while abandoning others and hoping we're right. And we certainly don't want to base our understanding of Scripture on the beliefs of our culture rather than the other way around.

Thankfully, there's a better way to understand the Bible than skipping over the parts we don't understand, reinterpreting the parts we don't like, and following only the parts *we* deem acceptable.

While we will likely never fully understand every command we see in Scripture, we can dramatically increase our chances of correctly understanding the Bible's instruction if we consider the similarities and differences between when the words were originally written and when we're reading them now.

For example, we might ask ourselves questions such as:

- Did the events of this passage take place in the Old Testament or the New Testament?
- Had Jesus died on the cross yet?
- How much of the Old Testament law did the original audience have, know, and understand?
- How much of the gospel message did the original audience have, know, and understand?
- Did the original audience have the Holy Spirit to guide them?
- What were the cultural expectations, social norms, and societal pressures at the time?
- Does the Bible's command differ from the cultural expectations at that time? If so, how?

- What limitations did the original audience face
  that we don't today, and vice versa?

While you may not be able to answer all these questions, the more information you can learn about a passage, the better equipped you'll be to determine the original author's or speaker's intended message so you can figure out how each particular passage of Scripture might apply to *you*.

Many of these answers won't be found in the passage itself. You may need to reference additional portions of Scripture, the notes provided in your study Bible, a quality Bible handbook or history book, or multiple online commentaries, sermons, or articles.

It may be time consuming, but researching questions like these almost always offers greater insight into the meaning of the original text and how it may (or may not) apply within our current culture.

Let's look at another example together.

Dive Deeper into Scripture

→ Read Matthew 19:16–17. What did Jesus say the man must do to get eternal life? Compare this to John 3:16 and Ephesians 2:8–9. How do these verses say we gain eternal life?

→ What similarities exist between the rich man in Matthew 19 and us today? What differences exist? (Hint: Where is this story in the Bible in relation to Jesus' death and resurrection? What does the man's reaction in verses 18–22 tell us about his priorities, which Jesus would have known all along?)

→ Do you think Jesus' command in verse 17b still directly
   applies to us? Why or why not? If not, what main idea
   should we get from this passage? (Hint: Make sure it
   passes all five tests above!)

7. Figure Out How You Can Live Out God's Principles Today

Have you ever heard the statement, "God said it. I believe it. That
settles it"? Perhaps you've even said it yourself. Unfortunately, as
we've seen in this chapter, obeying God's Word isn't always as easy or
straightforward as we'd like.

This is because Jesus doesn't ask us to follow a long list of strict
rules and clear guidelines. He asks us to follow *Him* … to learn more
about who He is, what He values, and what He wants so we can
model our lives after His.

This reminds me of an incident that happened shortly after I
received my learner's permit.

One of the first places I was allowed to drive on my own was
to a small choir performance halfway across town. I drove there
without problem, but when it was time to go, I noticed one of my
classmates I didn't know well still hanging around. He didn't have
a ride home.

Technically, I wasn't allowed to drive him. I only had a learner's
permit. But I clearly remember asking myself, *What would my dad
do in this situation?*

This was before I had a cell phone, so I couldn't call and ask. And
nearly everyone else had gone, so I couldn't ask a friend. Instead, I
had to rely on what I already knew about my dad, what he values,
and the types of choices he typically makes.

When I arrived home, I immediately told my dad about my decision. "I know I'm not supposed to drive other people yet, but he didn't have another way home … It felt like the right thing to do."

Thankfully, my dad wasn't upset at all. He was happy to see I made it home safe and relieved to learn I had only driven a classmate home—not a random man on the side of the road, as he had initially misunderstood! (That would have been a hard no.)

So what would your heavenly Father want *you* to do in the situations you're facing? Do you know God well enough to know what He's like, what types of choices He makes, and what He values?

If not, I'd invite you to get to know Him through the pages of His Word.

The Bible may not give you an exact answer for the specific situation you're facing, but the more you know God, His character, and His values, the better equipped you'll be to ask yourself, *What would my heavenly Father want me to do in this situation?*

Dive Deeper into Scripture

→ Read Psalm 103:1–14. What does this psalm tell us about God's character? List ten adjectives describing what God is like.

4

Hearing God's Spoken Word

Where is God leading me personally?

Recently, one of my children told me he's worried because he doesn't know his purpose in life. Why did God create him specifically, and what does God want him to do?

I lovingly assured him, "You're still a kid—you're not supposed to know your overall life purpose yet! Your purpose *right now* is to love God, love others, and do well in school so you'll be prepared for whatever God might call you to in the future. And that's exactly what you're doing." Thankfully, this seemed to ease his concerns.

Over the last few chapters, we've looked to Scripture to uncover God's will for all Christians in general.

We learned that the two most important commands in all of Scripture are to love God and love others. We learned that Jesus asks all of us to repent, follow Him, believe in Him, and make disciples. And in the last chapter, we learned a seven-step framework we can use to help us figure out how the Bible's general commands for all believers might apply to our lives today.

At this point, you may still have the same questions my son did: What is God's will for *my* life personally? Why did He put me on this earth, and what does He want me to do?

Have you ever wrestled with questions like these?

Maybe you feel as though God is calling you to step out in faith, do something big, or start something new—but you're not sure if it's God's voice you're hearing or your own. Maybe you know exactly what God is calling you to do, but you're scared and procrastinating. Or maybe you're ready and excited to get started … if only you had *any* idea what God has for you to do next. You've prayed and prayed for wisdom and direction but heard nothing.

Maybe you think God calls only the lucky few—people who are smart, pretty, talented, funny, outgoing, or naturally motivated—not people like you. You're too young, too old, too busy, too loud, too quiet, too weird, or too average. Maybe you would love to make a difference for the kingdom, but you're convinced you're no one special, you have nothing to offer, or you don't have what it takes.

Maybe you have an illness or disability, you have children with special needs, you're barely making ends meet, or you don't have reliable transportation. Maybe you're a teen mom or a high-school dropout working a low-level job with no influence. Maybe you're too busy running your own company (that you started from scratch) to take on yet another project.

Recently, someone told me she can't do video because she has a southern accent. I *wish* I had a southern accent! I'd move to Tennessee in a heartbeat if I could. But that's not where God has called our family in this season.

Friend, you are not a mistake. God created you on purpose, to accomplish the mission He specifically created you to fulfill.

Of course you don't have the same personality, gifts, talents, or abilities as anyone else. God isn't asking you to be the best version of *them*. He's inviting you to live out the purpose He's given *you*! Please rest assured, **God has given and will give you everything you need to accomplish His will for your life**.

The question is, *What* is *God's will for your life?*

Dive Deeper into Scripture

→ Read Ephesians 2:10 and Psalm 139:13–16. Why were you created? When did God determine His plan for your life?

→ Read 1 Corinthians 12:4–11. How are our gifts determined? Why are we given these gifts (v. 7)?

Three Common Myths about God's Will

Before we seek to determine what God's will *is*, we first need to address what God's will is *not*. Here are three common myths that can prevent us from discerning God's will for our lives.

Myth 1: God Only Has One Will for Your Entire Life

Remember in the introduction to this chapter, when I told my son, "Your purpose *right now* is to … do well in school so you'll be prepared for whatever God might call you to in the future"?

While we often focus on finding the one big purpose God put us on this earth to fulfill, God often calls us to multiple roles and responsibilities throughout our lives.

In fact, God's will for your life will likely look very different when you're ten than when you're twenty, forty, sixty, or eighty.

Just because God hasn't given you one huge, impressive mission to accomplish *right now* doesn't mean you aren't living out God's will for your life in this season. There may be opportunities right in front of you that you simply haven't noticed (more on this in the next chapter), you may be in a season of preparation, or it simply may not be time yet.

Rather than worrying about missing your "one big calling," ask yourself, *How can I serve God well in this season, with the resources and abilities I have right now?*

Myth 2: God's Will Always Involves a Big Decision

While it's certainly appropriate to seek God's will in the big decisions (where to live, who to marry, which job to take, etc.), sometimes God also gives us special short-term assignments we can complete within our everyday lives.

This happened to me a few weeks ago. I was taking the pup for a walk (as I often do) when I noticed a young woman being slowly followed by a man in a car. She was clearly upset, but she wasn't showing any signs of fear. A few minutes later, the man drove away.

I felt like I should go check on her. I didn't hear the voice of God or feel a strong sense of urgency; I simply wanted to make sure she was okay. It felt like the right thing to do.

Thankfully, she was okay. We sat and talked for over an hour, and I had the opportunity to pray with her, to share some hard-won advice and perspective from my own life, to remind her that God still loves her, and to point her back to Christ.

I'll probably never know how her situation turned out, but I'm so thankful I took a leap of faith to ask a total stranger, "Are you okay?" and "Can I pray for you?"

What special short-term assignment might the Holy Spirit be asking you to complete? Don't overlook small opportunities to follow God's will and make a big impact!

Myth 3: God's Will Is Super Spiritual, Difficult, or Weird

If, at this point, you're thinking, *I could* never *walk up to a stranger and ask to pray for her!* that's perfectly okay. While God does call some Christians to become pastors, priests, missionaries, or even individuals brave enough to pray for strangers in public, God's will for our lives isn't always super spiritual, difficult, or weird.

Have you ever randomly felt prompted to text a friend, send a check, write a card, say a prayer, speak up, get involved, or avoid a specific place or circumstance? If so, it may have been the Holy Spirit at work.

These small promptings can be easy to miss, since they typically sound like our own thoughts and ideas, but why not ask God and then follow them? The Holy Spirit may have something special planned, and you don't want to miss out!

Dive Deeper into Scripture

→ Read Jeremiah 29:4–7. What does the Lord command the Israelites to do in this passage? Which of the myths above does this passage refute?

→ Read Mark 14:12–16. What did the disciples find? How
did it get that way? Which of these myths does this
passage refute?

One Sunday afternoon, after listening to a sermon at church,
I felt compelled to ask God, "What do You want from me in
this life?" As I listened, I heard His still, small voice in my
heart saying, "Worship Me." I felt peaceful with His answer.

I don't have the gift of music or the charisma to preach,
but I do have a will to please my God. So I worship by being
attentive to my child and husband, by offering hospitality
and generosity when it's needed, and by returning to God's
presence and His Word as often as possible. This is how I
live out God's will for my life.

How to Hear God's Voice

As Christians, we believe God still actively speaks and guides us today
through the third person of the Trinity, the Holy Spirit. (Whether we
talk about hearing God's voice or hearing from the Holy Spirit—it's
the same concept.) But this doesn't mean hearing God's voice is
always easy or straightforward.

So you may be wondering, *What does God's voice sound like?*

For me (and most people I've talked to), God's voice typically
sounds like my own voice in my head, but different. Alternately, I

might feel a strong sense to do or say something. Or I might even feel God giving me a raised-eyebrow "look" from heaven, the same way I might sense a friend giving me a similar look here on earth.

Sometimes I hear God's voice while I'm praying. Other times He chimes in throughout the day to remind me of a Bible verse, to convict me of my sin, to encourage me to make a wise decision, or to draw my attention to something He doesn't want me to miss.

Sometimes, when I'm reading my Bible, it's as if the words practically leap off the page. I might hear Him whisper in my soul, "That [specific application] doesn't apply to you. I'm not calling you there." Or, "Notice My character here. I don't change. I'm going to come through for you too."

My absolute favorite memory of hearing God speak took place while I was running barefoot along the beach in Florida at sunrise. (Talk about a time to meet with God!) As I was pouring my heart out in prayer while simultaneously looking out over the beautiful expanse of endless ocean waves, I clearly heard God make two specific promises I've held on to ever since.

But that doesn't mean God's voice is always so clear.

When I was a teenager, God's voice sounded distant, vague, and quiet. What I now know was God's guidance and direction initially felt like a random thought or idea that would probably never happen. I remember thinking, *Who, me? How could I do anything special? I'm nobody.*

Now, God's voice typically sounds close, familiar, and clear … in part because I've been intentionally practicing hearing (and obeying) God's voice for more than two decades. I can't wait to find out what it will be like after I've followed God for eighty years!

This is how I typically hear from God, both now and in the past, but these certainly aren't the only ways God speaks to us.

Hebrews 1:1 states, "In the past God spoke to our ancestors through the prophets at many times and in various ways." For example, God spoke to Joseph through dreams,[1] Moses through a burning bush,[2] Balaam through a talking donkey,[3] Elijah through a gentle whisper,[4] and Peter and Paul through visions.[5]

Today God most often speaks to us through:

- **His Word:** A certain verse may pop out at us when we read our Bibles, or God may call a verse to mind throughout the day (2 Tim. 3:16; Heb. 4:12).

- **Prayer:** When we speak to God in prayer, we may sense Him responding to us—not as an audible voice but in our thoughts or spirits (1 Cor. 2:9–16).

- **Our thoughts:** This is similar to hearing God in prayer, except we don't have to be praying first in order to hear God speak (1 Cor. 2:10).

- **Our conscience:** We may feel deeply convicted in our hearts that something is wrong or right, despite not having a specific Bible verse to back up our convictions (Rom. 2:14–15).

- **Our feelings or desires:** God may place a strong emotion or desire on our hearts as a way of guiding us toward a specific path or action (Phil. 2:13).

- **Our circumstances:** God may guide our decisions by closing one door and opening another (Acts 16:6–10).
- **Other people:** God may prompt people we know to give us advice (whether solicited or unsolicited, knowingly or unknowingly) that confirms, denies, or leads us toward a particular calling (Ezek. 2:1–4).

Additionally, God can also speak to us through dreams,[6] visions,[7] nature,[8] supernatural signs and miracles,[9] or even an audible voice,[10] though these methods aren't as common.

Dive Deeper into Scripture

→ Read I Samuel 3:4–10. How does God speak to Samuel here? Why didn't Samuel recognize the Lord's voice at first?

→ Read 2 Samuel 12:1–15. What are two ways God spoke to King David after his affair with Bathsheba? How did King David respond to God's message?

God's Guidance in Buying a Home

My husband and I recently experienced God's direction in a very tangible way. We decided we were ready to move out of our cramped starter house and into a bigger one in a neighborhood where our kids could grow up around other kids their age.

Knowing what a big decision this was, I started praying, "God, please help us find the perfect home for us. And if it isn't the perfect home, please make sure the deal falls through."

We casually browsed online home-buying apps for about a year and a half before we finally found a house we were really excited about.

Now, at the time, houses in our area were selling *really* fast—sometimes within hours of listing and often well over asking price—but this house had been on the market for more than three weeks. We drove by several times, told our friends and family about it, and put in a fair offer, fully expecting to have it accepted.

We waited all weekend for an official answer, only to learn they'd decided to sell to someone else.

No big deal. I had been praying that if this house wasn't God's will for us, the deal wouldn't work out, and it didn't. So we kept looking.

This happened a second time. And a third time. Every time we found a home we liked (that had been on the market for weeks), either it immediately sold to someone else or the owner flat-out rejected our offer.

We were definitely noticing a pattern, but we weren't worried. Instead, I continued to pray, "God, please help us find the perfect home for us. And if it isn't the perfect home, please make sure the deal falls through."

Then we found a brand-new listing I absolutely *loved*. And this time, our offer was accepted almost immediately. The seller didn't wait for multiple offers or try to start a bidding war (even though he easily could have). He chose us.

If our home-buying plans had fallen through once, we would have chalked it up to coincidence. But *three* outright rejections on what should have been easy sales, followed by an immediate yes on a perfect, in-demand home we didn't expect to get? It was clear God was at work.

If only God's guidance were always so clear!

Dive Deeper into Scripture

→ Read Judges 6:36–40. How does God confirm His will for Gideon in this passage? Should we expect the same sign today? Why or why not?

→ Read Matthew 3:13–17 and Luke 7:20–23. What signs had John already seen and heard to indicate who Jesus really was? Why do you think he still asked for confirmation?

How to Know If It's Really God Talking to You

So how can we know if God is truly speaking to us or if something is merely a coincidence, our own idea, or—worse—Satan trying to trick us?

It can be difficult to know with 100 percent certainty where each of our thoughts comes from. This is why 1 Thessalonians 5:21 instructs us to "test them all; hold on to what is good." We don't want to assume something is God's will if it isn't.

Thankfully, we don't have to blindly guess. Here are a few questions you can use to help you determine if you're truly hearing God's voice or just your own:

- Does the thought, idea, or action line up with Scripture?
- Does it make sense in light of what God has already asked you to do?
- Is it true and logical?
- Does it contribute to the good of yourself and others?
- Does it honor God or only yourself?
- What are the likely outcomes or consequences of each choice?
- Does it make sense in light of your past experiences?
- Does it line up with your current personality, gifts, and abilities?
- Does it lead to conviction and growth or to shame and condemnation?[11]
- Have godly mentors confirmed this call in your life?

Now, God's will doesn't have to pass *all* of these tests. God might be calling you to pursue a new role in this season, or He might ask you to do something that doesn't make sense from a worldly perspective.

But God will *never* call you to do something that's clearly immoral, that goes against Scripture, that is likely to lead you into sin or harm your relationship with Him, or that doesn't make *any* sense in light of your current knowledge, gifts, and abilities.

Dive Deeper into Scripture

→ Read Exodus 2:1–10; 3:7–10. What was God's call on Moses's life? How does this call compare to the questions above? How was Moses uniquely positioned to answer God's call?

→ Read Esther 2:2–7, 17–18; 3:1, 5–6; 4:7–14. What did Mordecai want Esther to do? How does Esther's call compare to the questions above? How was Esther uniquely positioned to fulfill this role?

→ Read Hosea 1:2–3; 3:1. What was God's call on Hosea's life? How does Hosea's call compare to the questions above? Did Hosea behave immorally? What was the intended effect of this calling?

Roberta's Story

One night at a Bible study in 2012, I felt a call from God to start a women's group in our church. I checked with several of the women and the pastor to find out their opinions. Some women seemed excited, and others said it had been tried before and it didn't/wouldn't work.

I did a lot of praying and asking God to help me with this project. We are a very small church, so with the help from another lady and God, we went ahead with the plans to give it a try. We decided that even if just three or four showed up, we would have it.

Since the beginning, we are still going strong with several in attendance. We do cheer baskets—flowers or other gifts for occasions such as new babies, illness, appreciation, and just "thinking of you." We do fundraisers and freewill offerings for the expenses of all our activities. We have set up an active prayer group on Facebook.

I continually pray to God, thanking Him for this group and for all He does for us.

Reasons You Might Not Hear from God

Time and time again, the Bible assures us that we are not alone and that God will lead us, guide us, and speak to us through the Holy Spirit.

This is why John 14:16–17 tells us, "And I will ask the Father, and he will give you another advocate to help you and be with you forever—the Spirit of truth. The world cannot accept him, because it neither sees him nor knows him. But you know him, for *he lives with you and will be in you.*"

Similarly, John 16:13 tells us, "But when he, the Spirit of truth, comes, *he will guide you into all the truth.* He will not speak on his own; he will speak only what he hears, and he will tell you what is yet to come."

However, what happens when you seek God's will and you don't hear anything? As frustrating as it can be to pray for answers only to hear silence in return, it does happen. Here are seven reasons you might struggle to hear God's voice.

1. You Haven't Asked

What do you typically do first when you have a tough decision to make?

Do you ask friends and family for advice? Do you read books, blogs, or articles for more information to help you make the right call? Do you simply try things until you find what works? Or do you immediately ask God for wisdom?

While it's perfectly appropriate to read books, to take personality tests, spiritual gifts inventories, and career aptitude tests, and to ask godly friends and mentors for advice when seeking God's will for your life, you don't want to forget to ask the Holy Spirit for wisdom, clarity, and direction as well.

After all, not only is God the only one who has all the answers, but He truly *wants* to help us find and follow His will for our lives.

This is why James 4:2b reminds us, "You do not have because you do not ask God."

This verse doesn't mean that God will always give us everything we ask for. But sometimes the reason we don't have the answers we want is simply because we haven't taken the time to ask.

Dive Deeper into Scripture

→ Read James 1:5 and Proverbs 2:6. Why should we seek God's will in prayer?

2. You Haven't Taken the Time to Listen

After you've taken the time to talk *to* God in prayer, you'll also want to set aside time to listen for a response *from* God as well.

God's voice can often be quiet or subtle. And it's hard to hear God's wisdom and direction if you're constantly filling your mind with noise from books, TV, social media, or conversations with friends and family rather than listening for Him to speak.

Dive Deeper into Scripture

→ Read Exodus 3:1–4. What might have happened if Moses had decided he was too busy tending the sheep to check out the burning bush?

3. You Need to Be Patient

You may have noticed: God doesn't always answer our prayers for wisdom and direction right away.

He may be putting details into place that you know nothing about, He may have you in a season of preparation so you're ready for whatever He has next, or He may have a special assignment for you right now where you're at.

Don't be so anxious to rush on to the next thing that you completely miss what God is doing *now*. What might God be teaching you in this season? How might He be preparing you now for what He'll ask you to do next? Maybe right where you are is right where you need to be.

Dive Deeper into Scripture

→ Read Genesis 12:1–7. How old was Abraham before he heard God's call for his life? Read Genesis 21:1–5. How long did Abraham and Sarah have to wait until God's promise of an heir was fulfilled?

4. You Have Heard from God, but You Didn't Realize It

While God certainly can speak to us through a loud, booming voice or through a sequence of undeniable miracles, His guidance is usually far more subtle. Think through the thoughts, ideas, coincidences, opportunities, and circumstances you've experienced lately. Could one of them have been a prompting from the Holy Spirit that you initially overlooked or didn't realize was from the Lord?

Dive Deeper into Scripture

→ Read Numbers 22:21–34. How does God speak to Balaam in this passage? How does Balaam initially misinterpret this unusual sign?

5. You Heard God, but You Refused to Listen

Alternately, perhaps you did hear God, but you didn't like what you heard.

If God has asked you to repent of a specific sin, remove yourself from a questionable relationship, or follow Him into something new, don't wait for Him to tell you something different.

Not only does God rarely change His plan, but God often expects each of us to obey Him in what He has *already* asked us to do (no matter how big or small) before He gives us additional information or next steps.

Where might God still be waiting for you to obey today?

Dive Deeper into Scripture

→ Read Jonah 1:1–4, 11–12, 15, 17. What did God tell Jonah to do? What happened when he disobeyed?

→ Read Jonah 3:1–5. Did God give Jonah a different call? What happened when Jonah finally obeyed?

6. It Isn't Time Yet

As human beings with limited knowledge and insight, we don't always know what needs and opportunities tomorrow may hold, but we can rest assured that God does.

God may have something new and exciting He's waiting to reveal to you, but it simply isn't time yet. Or He may have you right where you are right now for a reason.

Not every season of our lives has to hold amazing kingdom work or exciting spiritual adventures as the world sees it. Sometimes God's will for our lives is simply for us to love Him—and others—where we are until He calls us somewhere else. That's a wonderful assignment as well.

Dive Deeper into Scripture

→ Read Genesis 5:32; 6:11–14. Approximately how old was Noah when he first heard God's call for his life? What do you think Noah did before this? (Hint: The Bible doesn't say.)

7. God Has Given You Freedom to Decide for Yourself

When my children get dressed in the morning, they have a few general rules to follow.

They must wear clean underwear every day. They must wear long pants and closed-toed shoes in January. They cannot wear swimsuits to church or church clothes to the pool. Their clothes must be at least relatively clean, modest, and appropriate for wherever they're headed.

I will not change my mind on any of these rules (no matter how much they argue). Within these rules, however, they have a great deal of freedom to make decisions for themselves. Whether they want to wear the red shirt, the blue shirt, the polka dot shirt, or the dinosaur shirt, any of these choices are okay with me.

It's the same with God.

As we saw in chapters 1–3, God has provided some very important rules and guidelines for our lives that He expects us to obey. Within these commands, however, there is a great deal of freedom.

Maybe God is calling you to a specific location, profession, or relationship. Or maybe He's simply calling you to love Him and His people well wherever you are. There's no need to overspiritualize every decision or put that much pressure on yourself to figure everything out.

If you don't know where God is calling you right now, that's okay. Obey the commands and instructions you have been given (there are plenty in the Bible!), and be open to wherever God might call you next, even if that's simply right where you are now.

As Christians, our job isn't necessarily to actively "discover" God's will for our lives if we don't feel satisfied where we are currently. Rather, **God simply asks us to obey Him where He has us, trusting Him to guide us to our next steps in His perfect timing**.

5

Finding Opportunities to Serve

How can I make a difference right where I am?

"Brittany, how did you know that starting Equipping Godly Women was God's will for your life?"

I've been asked this question a few times now, and it always makes me smile. It seems to imply that either I received a definitive sign at some point or I followed an easy five-step process that gave me the exact clarity I needed. However, figuring out God's plan for your life is rarely that simple or straightforward.

Honestly, I had no idea that starting Equipping Godly Women was God's will for my life. I originally went to college to become a research psychologist.

The Christian university I chose to attend had a strong missions focus, so I quickly found ways to get involved in my local community. I signed up to teach third-grade Sunday school after hearing about the need during morning announcements, and I volunteered to help teach a Wednesday night program at a nearby inner-city church after another student offered me a ride.

Because of these two amazing opportunities, I quickly fell in love with teaching. I switched my major to elementary education with the hope of becoming a middle school language arts teacher in an inner-city public school. But that's not what happened next.

Instead, the summer before my senior year, I moved to Nashville to pursue my dream of becoming a famous country singer. My time in Music City was short, but I will never forget the thrill of being up onstage, singing my little heart out as the crowd sang along. It was nothing short of magical.

Then, within months, everything changed again. As I shared in my previous book, *Fall in Love with God's Word*, when I found out I was pregnant, my life was dramatically altered overnight. I went from a girl who could hop in a car and experience Nashville nightlife on a whim to one who was now stuck at home with a newborn while my new husband worked out of town all week to make ends meet.

I was convinced I'd ruined God's plan for my life—whatever it was. I messed up. I got pregnant. And now it was just me, the baby, endless piles of laundry, more medical bills than I knew what to do with, and no idea how any of it would turn out. Little did I know, this was exactly where I needed to be for what God had planned for me.

Three diaper-filled years later, shortly after the arrival of our second little one, I happened to read a blog post that recommended ghostwriting online articles as a way to earn money from home. The topics were awful and the pay was pitiful, but we had hospital bills to pay, and I wasn't doing anything during naptime anyway. I signed up and started writing.

A few months later, my sister-in-law started a blog, so I started one too. I thought it would be a fun hobby—something I could do during naptime. I had *no* idea it would ever turn into anything more. And yet, here we are today.

Currently, Equipping Godly Women is a popular Christian women's website, reaching millions of women in nearly every country in the world. I've written eight books, hosted online women's conferences that have drawn in thousands, and been featured on Christian radio as well as in several major online publications. It's been quite the ride!

Eight years ago, if you had asked me what I thought God's plan for my life was, I wouldn't have been able to tell you. Everything I'd done until that point felt so disconnected. Research psychology ... teaching ... moving to Nashville ... getting pregnant ... ghostwriting medical articles ... It all felt very random, and I couldn't see God's plan in any of it.

Yet, looking back now, it all makes perfect sense. I never became a research psychologist, a classroom teacher, or a famous country singer. But I see God was using every one of these experiences—as disjointed as they felt at the time—to prepare me for the writing and speaking career I'm building now. I had no idea how my life would turn out, but God knew all along.

All this to say, just because you don't see God's plan now doesn't mean He doesn't have one. It only means He hasn't fully revealed it to you yet. The people, opportunities, and circumstances all around you may very well be actively preparing you for whatever God might call you to next.

So what do you do when you *want* to follow God's will for your life, you've prayed and sought His direction, and you've done your best to live out His commands but you still have no idea what God wants you to do?

The answer is easy: you try things!

If God hasn't explicitly told you "Do this" or "Don't do this," you're free to pursue any hobbies, interests, or opportunities you like. What sounds fun or interesting to you?

Dive Deeper into Scripture

→ Read Exodus 3:1–10; 7:7. Approximately how old was Moses when he heard God's call on his life? What was he doing before this?

→ Read Acts 9:1–6. What was Paul doing when he received God's call on his life? Then read Galatians 1:13–14. How had God already begun preparing Paul for his work as a missionary and New Testament author long before he became a Christian?

What Opportunities Are Available to You?

When I signed up to start ghostwriting medical articles, I truly had no long-term plan, much less a spiritual one. I wasn't planning on becoming a professional writer (and certainly not in the medical field). I simply wanted to pay our debt down faster. That was all I knew at the time.

While we may think we have to know exactly what God wants us to do or have our plans mapped out in advance, that's rarely the case. In my experience, God gently leads us one step at a time, often through the circumstances, situations, and opportunities all around us.

In this chapter, we're looking at five ways you can take advantage of the existing opportunities around you to serve others, whether that's through a job, a relationship, a volunteer position, a conversation, or simply a good deed.

Who knows? One of these suggestions might just help you figure out where God is calling you next. But even if it doesn't, you'll still be actively fulfilling what Jesus tells us are the two most important commands of all: loving God and loving others.

I. Be on the Lookout for Existing Opportunities

If you've attended church or read your Bible for any length of time, you're probably familiar with the story of the good Samaritan in Luke 10:25–37.

In this parable, a priest, a Levite, and a Samaritan are all presented with an opportunity to help a man lying half-dead on the side of the road. Both the priest and the Levite walk right past the man; only the Samaritan stops to help.

While we all know we're supposed to be like the good Samaritan in this story, how many times do we ignore the needs of those around us?

Sure, we can't help everyone. We aren't called to. (Even Jesus didn't heal everyone He met.)[1] Yet how often do we miss opportunities to serve simply because we aren't paying attention?

Can you volunteer to coach your kids' sports teams, organize the church bake sale, or cook a meal for a family in need? Can you donate your gently used clothes and toys to a women's shelter, purchase extra school supplies for neighborhood schools, or write letters to soldiers overseas? Can you sponsor a child, play with puppies at the local animal shelter, or knit baby blankets for infants in intensive care?

Serving others doesn't have to be complicated, expensive, or time-consuming. What opportunities are right in front of you? Why not sign up and see where it leads?

Dive Deeper into Scripture

→ Read the story of the good Samaritan in Luke 10:25–37. While Scripture doesn't tell us for sure, why do you think the priest and Levite might have walked right by? Why might people still walk by the needs all around them today?

Ann's Story

After my first year in church, I was asked to share my testimony in a women's correctional facility. I was hesitant at first, but it was a clear call from God, so I obeyed.

A year later, I heard God say, "Share the gospel with the prisoners." I said, "Lord, can we do this some other time?" But of course, I got myself ready.

A few months later, with the help of two other ladies, I started a ministry teaching Bible studies in the jail every Saturday.

Since then, more than a thousand inmates have joined our weekly Bible studies, and 176 of them have been baptized. We've also been training leaders so the women can continue to do Bible studies even without us. When the jails were under lockdown during the quarantine in 2020, the women were still able to do Bible studies on their own.

I'm so thankful I listened to God's call to start a women's prison ministry when I did.

2. Assess Your Knowledge, Skills, and Abilities

Is there anything you're especially good at? Do you have any skills or abilities the average person doesn't have? Have you been through something that gave you unique knowledge, perspective, or experience? If so, how can you use these skills or experiences to help others in need?

Can you paint, teach geometry, write, clean, solve tech issues, play the guitar, run a sound machine, run a half marathon, organize people for a cause, write letters, make phone calls, or run errands? Can you give business, parenting, marriage, life, or career advice?

Do you have experience negotiating contracts, reducing medical debt, parenting a child with special needs, rebuilding a marriage after infidelity, coping with mental illness, recovering from an eating disorder, or escaping abuse? Would you be willing to share your story with others?

Don't limit yourself to only your professional skills or to skills no one else has. Even if you consider yourself only marginally talented in a specific area, chances are, someone would appreciate your perspective. God gave you your experience, knowledge, talents, and abilities to share with others. Don't keep them to yourself!

Dive Deeper into Scripture

→ Read 1 Corinthians 12:12–27. Why does God give us all different gifts, knowledge, talents, and abilities? What happens if we don't share them with others?

→ Read 2 Corinthians 1:3–7. Why does God allow, and then comfort us in, our troubles?

Dawna's Story

For years, I was abused, stalked, and beaten to a pulp on a regular basis. As a result, I suffered two strokes and was unable to work. My four children and I wound up sleeping on mattresses in the basement of a family member's house. It felt like a dungeon.

Through this difficult time, I clung to God and His Word for dear life, and I prayed, "God, please save us from this dungeon and help us be approved for housing!" Two hours later, I read my daily devotional. It said, "God's smile in a dungeon is better than His frown in a palace." Amazing!

Romans 8:28 promises us, "And we know that in all things God works for the good of those who love him, who have been called according to his purpose." I clung to this verse, believing that God would keep His promise.

Later that day, I went to the mailbox and found an approval letter for Section 8 government housing. We were able to move back into the same house we had moved out of five months earlier! I knew God was keeping His promise to me.

After this, I became highly involved at my church. We regularly go out to minister to addicts, women in bad situations, and the homeless, and I teach a women's ministry, which I started in my living room.

Because of my past, I wasn't sure I could do this. Yet, it's because of my roughness and my past experiences that I'm able to strengthen and encourage other women that they can overcome their circumstances too. I can show women how to love, trust, and obey God—no matter what else is happening in their lives.

God kept His promise to me, and He will keep His promises to you too!

3. Use Your Interests and Hobbies to Serve Others

As we discussed earlier, following God's will for your life doesn't have to be only spiritual or challenging. What if you could pursue His call for you simply by doing something you love?

Do you enjoy watching movies with friends? What if you mentored an at-risk teenager or helped with your church's youth group? What if you started a website with TV and movie reviews to help

Christian parents make educated choices about their children's screen time? Do you love scrapbooking, knitting, sketching, studying the Bible, or researching genealogies? What if you offered to teach classes at your local nursing home?

Alternately, what if you used these skills to start your own small business and then you donated a portion of the proceeds to help your favorite charity? (This is what we do at Equipping Godly Women!)

Rather than signing up for something new, you might simply look for ways you can use your existing hobbies and interests to make a difference.

Dive Deeper into Scripture

→ Read I Corinthians 10:31. What types of activities does this passage tell us to glorify God in? How can our normal, everyday tasks (grocery shopping, washing dishes, paying the bills) bring glory to God?

→ Read I Peter 4:10–11. What does this passage say we should do with our gifts?

Jennifer's Story

I never expected God to lead me to become a full-time writer at the age of forty-four. While I'd always been an avid reader and dabbled in creative journaling and poetry, I thought becoming an author was a far-fetched dream that would never be realized.

Then, as my kids got older and left home, I started to feel like there was something more waiting around the corner. I prayed for God to lead me in His will for my life, and He surprised me with a clear prompting to write a women's Bible study.

Even though my mind was full of insecurities, I obediently studied the Scriptures, prayed for guidance, and began to write. A few months later, I submitted the completed manuscript to my church leadership. Then, a few days later, I got a call from one of the pastors saying they had reviewed my study and would love for me to begin leading it at church!

I was nervous that no one would choose my study but pleasantly surprised to see the class fill up quickly. Eventually, I expanded my writing endeavors to various ministries and online outreaches.

Now I'm only days away from turning fifty, and I've never felt more in line with God's will for my life.

4. Meet an Existing Need

Do you or anyone in your family or community have a specific hardship? Are there any services or resources you wish you had access to (either currently or in the past)? Are there other women, children, or families who could benefit from a solution to this problem as well? If so, is there a way you could help meet this need, both for yourself and others?

Can you trade childcare with a friend or set up a Moms' Night Out for families in your neighborhood? Can you clean a local park, organize a meal swap, set up an after-school tutoring program, or start a job-training program in your area? Can you create an extensive list of resources for families with autism in your area? Can you figure out a way to get better childcare options for everyone at your office?

Chances are, if there's a resource you wish you had (either currently or in the past), someone else wishes they had it as well. Why not figure out how to create that resource yourself?

Dive Deeper into Scripture

→ Read Galatians 6:2 and Acts 2:42–47. How would our lives and our experience of Christianity be different if all Christians shared one another's burdens in the ways named in these verses?

→ Read Ecclesiastes 4:9–12. What benefits can partnering together with other believers offer us (both from this passage and your own experience)?

Christy's Story

When the homeschool hybrid program our family had been a part of began making changes, another mother and I felt called to establish a different option.

Within weeks, we secured a low-cost location, a priest advisor to give us weekly mass, several amazing tutors, and a group of families ready to sign up.

Our group grew threefold in one year as we expanded to offer a Friday speaker series, hosted parent activities, and partnered with an area school district for supplemental opportunities and funding.

Looking back on the whirlwind of origination and execution, we know it was only through the power of the Holy Spirit that we were able to accomplish what we did.

5. Ask Around to See How You Can Help

"In our family, everyone helps." This is a phrase I repeat often, as I ask my children to help with the dishes, laundry, groceries, and more. "Mom is not the maid."

Yes, it's nice to have my family's help getting the chores done. But even more, I want to raise children who habitually seek to serve those around them, both in big ways and in small. And I want to be that kind of person myself.

This is why our family gives a neighborhood girl a ride to school with us every morning. It's no trouble for us (we're headed there anyway), and it really helps her family.

We regularly donate canned goods, school supplies, diapers, old toys, and baby clothes to local organizations that can use them. We shoveled our elderly neighbor's driveway after the last big snowstorm, raked our other neighbors' leaves when their child was in the hospital, and brought several meals to families who have had babies or surgeries. And many others have done the same for us.

None of these actions are difficult, expensive, or time-consuming. **Sometimes the hardest part of helping our neighbors is simply slowing down enough to notice the needs all around us and lend a helping hand.**

Jodie's Story

My husband and I had only been married for a few years, and we were barely making it financially. During this time, our church needed to expand to accommodate their growing numbers, so they started a building program and asked the church members to give over and above their tithe for this expansion.

Through prayer, we knew that God was calling us to double our tithe. It was a little scary, and we weren't sure how this was going to work out, but we did it anyway.

Right after that, my manager called me into his office. He told me that the women engineers' salaries were increasing to match the male engineers' salaries. Then he gave me a paper with the new salary. I was shocked and thankful to see they doubled my salary! God is abundantly amazing!

Is there anyone in your life who could use your help today? Do you know any single dads, moms of children with special needs, or anyone facing job loss or food insecurity? Do you know any widows, any families facing significant medical or financial concerns, or anyone who has recently lost a friend or family member?

If not, you might discreetly ask your pastor or your children's school principal if they know anyone who could use some help. Alternately, you might do an online search for local nonprofits in your area that could benefit from your time, talent, or donations.

Keep your eye out for opportunities, and don't be afraid to reach out. You never know when God might use you as a huge blessing to someone else.

Dive Deeper into Scripture

→ Read Matthew 25:34–40. Who receives a reward in this passage?

→ Read James 1:22–27. What does this passage instruct us to do (and not do)? What are we promised if we follow through (v. 25)?

I hope this chapter has given you several ideas for ways you can serve others in your community and make a difference in the lives of those around you.

If you're still not sure, however, don't worry. Continue to ask around, keep your eyes open for new opportunities, and don't be afraid to try new things.

As I shared in the introduction of this chapter, I had no idea that running Equipping Godly Women was God's larger will for my life—until I was already doing it. I didn't go in with a huge plan or lots of clarity. I simply pursued an opportunity that sounded fun, and then God opened doors from there.

He can do the same for you as well.

6

Making Wise Decisions

What would God want me to do in this situation?

Have you ever said or done something you later regretted?

Maybe you made a one-time decision that had life-altering consequences. You lied, cheated, had an abortion, dropped out of school, or walked out on your marriage. You listened to the wrong advice, quit your job, gave in to temptation, said something you shouldn't have, or ruined a relationship.

Or maybe you made a series of small decisions whose consequences compounded over time. You weren't the mom you wanted to be. You stayed in a toxic relationship when you knew you should leave. You neglected your faith, your marriage, your health, your friendships, or your finances. And now you're reaping the consequences.

According to various online sources, American adults make as many as thirty-five thousand decisions each day.[1] While most of them are fairly inconsequential, you and I both know that one wrong choice can dramatically alter your life forever.

In fact, the Bible is full of examples of men and women who made poor choices and later suffered the consequences.

Adam and Eve chose to eat the fruit, causing the fall of mankind.[2] The Israelites repeatedly turned to idol worship, incurring God's wrath.[3] Moses disobeyed God's instruction and was prevented from entering the long-awaited Promised Land.[4] Samson allowed himself to be seduced by Delilah, leading to his immediate capture by the enemy army.[5] King David slept with a married woman, murdered her husband to cover it up, and lost their child as a result.[6]

Ananias and Sapphira lied to the apostles and were immediately struck dead.[7] Judas betrayed Jesus for thirty pieces of silver, then later hung himself.[8] And Peter denied Jesus three times before weeping bitterly over what he had done.[9]

Every single day, we're faced with an endless array of choices, many of which have the potential to dramatically change our lives or the lives of those around us, for better or for worse.

This is why it's so crucial that we learn to make wise decisions. Thankfully, we don't have to make them alone.

As we saw in the previous three chapters, God continues to give us a great deal of guidance through His written Word (the Bible), His spoken word (the Holy Spirit), and the opportunities all around us every day. Hopefully, these chapters have given you a few ideas of what God may be calling you to in this season or the next.

But what if you have multiple ideas and you're not sure which to pick? Or what if you aren't sure if an idea is actually God's will for your life or merely your own? How can you tell if a seemingly good decision is the right decision?

After all, God's will for our lives isn't always obvious.

For example, should you start a business, volunteer at a local nonprofit, or stay home with your children? Should you move to a new city or stay where you are? Which church should you attend? Should you cut ties with an old friend or stay in touch? None of these decisions are clearly immoral. So how do you choose?

Here are seven questions you can use (in order) to help you discern if a specific choice is in line with God's will for your life in this season.

I. Does the Bible Give an Explicit Command?

If the Bible gives a clear, explicit command, the answer is easy: Do what God has already commanded you to do in His Word. (And if you're not sure if God has given you an explicit command in this area, search Scripture to see.)

For example, you do not need to ask God if you should forgive,[10] respect your husband,[11] love others,[12] trust God,[13] or avoid evil.[14]

You don't need to ask all your friends and family for their opinion. You don't need to look for a sign or a loophole. And you don't need to pray for a different answer.

If God has already given you an answer in His Word, you simply need to obey.

2. Has God Already Given You Clear Direction?

Similarly, if God has already given you *clear* direction through the prompting of the Holy Spirit, you do not need to continue praying, hoping for a different answer. Again, you need to obey what He has already told you to do.

It's okay if you don't know all the details, you have no idea how it will all work out, or you're downright terrified. If God has called you to do something, He will guide you and equip you with everything you need to follow through.

Your job is simply to obey the direction you've been given so far, trusting that God will provide additional guidance and resources when you need them.

Dive Deeper into Scripture

→ Read 2 Peter 1:3–10. What role does God play in us fulfilling our life's calling? What role do we play?

→ Read Romans 11:29 and Exodus 4:10–16. Can we disqualify ourselves from God's call for our lives, due to past sin or doubt? Can we ask for a different call if we don't appreciate the one we are given? If not, what might we ask for instead?

3. Does This Decision Fit with God's Character?

Have you ever heard someone say, "I know what the Bible says, but surely God would want me to be happy"? Maybe you've even said it yourself.

While I do believe God wants us to be happy, this does not give us a free license to do whatever we want or whatever "feels right" at the time. True happiness and joy come from living out God's perfect will for our lives, and God would *never* ask or want us to behave in a way that is contrary to His character, His values, or His Word.

It's been years since the popular "What Would Jesus Do?" bracelets were all the rage, but the question is as relevant now as ever.

How would Jesus love your spouse, parent your children, treat your coworkers, or speak to others online? Would He yell, complain, manipulate, gossip, give the silent treatment, or speak poorly of others when they're not around? Or would He continually offer love, kindness, patience, and forgiveness to others, even when they don't deserve it?

When considering if a particular decision is in line with God's character, this simple filter might help: Would you feel comfortable sharing your decision with God, your godly husband, your religious grandma, or your entire church congregation? If not, that may be a sign you need to make a different choice.

Dive Deeper into Scripture

→ Read Psalm 116:5; Isaiah 40:28–31; and Micah 7:18–19. What do these verses tell us about God's character?

→ Read Galatians 5:16–23. Which types of behaviors result from walking according to the flesh? What fruit will we naturally produce when we walk according to the Holy Spirit?

4. Does This Choice Fit with Your Overall Life Narrative?

Sometimes I unintentionally frustrate my children by giving them too many conflicting instructions all at once.

For example, I might send them upstairs to brush their teeth, only to immediately call them back downstairs to clean up the mess they left behind or the chore they left undone. I might accidentally give them a job I don't realize they aren't old enough to handle, or I might mistakenly insist they find something that isn't there.

Thankfully, we don't have this same issue when God gives us guidance and direction.

While we humans can be scatterbrained or forgetful, God never asks us to do anything He hasn't first prepared us for, and He never gives us two tasks or roles we can't reasonably manage at the same time.

I love the story Michael Scanlan shares in his book *What Does God Want?*

> I attended a conference where a speaker talked about his own struggles to give his life fully to God. He had always been afraid to surrender completely to the Lord's will, he said, because he feared that the Lord would send him into the jungles of Africa—and that terrified him.… So he withheld part of himself.
>
> "Finally," the speaker said, "I did make a full commitment to the Lord despite my fears. And He didn't send me to Africa. I learned something—God never sends anyone to Africa without first putting Africa in his heart."[15]

Whether or not you know God's will for your life, God does. He's been busy preparing you over the course of your entire life, and He won't suddenly ask you to do something that conflicts with where He has already called you or how He has already equipped you.

Has God already called you to marriage or motherhood? Has He asked you to take care of a friend or family member with special needs, a severe health condition, or financial difficulties? Maybe you have a chronic health condition, your life feels crazy busy, or you're barely making ends meet yourself. None of these circumstances are a surprise to God.

Yes, God can certainly use anyone for anything, but He isn't likely to ask you to do something that makes *no* sense in light of your current interests, preferences, commitments, skills, and abilities.

Dive Deeper into Scripture

→ Read Ephesians 1:3–5; 2:10. When does God bless us, choose us, and prepare for us to do good works? What does this mean for the roles and responsibilities God hasn't called you to yet?

Stephanie's Story

I recently did a Bible study searching for my purpose. Through this study, I learned that my first calling, like everyone else, is to be a disciple of Christ.

My second calling was/is to let go of my job as a physical therapist and accept my role as a stay-at-home mom to my three children.

Instead of helping others heal physically, I'm called to help people heal by listening. Now I'm homeschooling my children and supporting those who are in need by texting and being there for them in their darkest moments. I know I'm living out my purpose, and I feel a sense of peace about it.

5. What Are Some Likely Outcomes of This Decision?

Whenever you find yourself stuck between two seemingly valid choices, a simple pros-and-cons list can come in very handy.

Start by making a list of all your options, and then consider the potential outcomes of each. How might each decision affect your faith, your family, your health, your life, and the lives of those around you? What's the best thing that could happen? What's the worst thing that could happen? Are these outcomes likely or unlikely?

Then take your questions one step deeper. Would this be a *wise* decision? Is it likely to lead you closer to God's best for your life, or further away? Do you feel God calling you in one direction or another, even if it isn't the easiest or most practical option?

It's okay if your decision doesn't make sense on paper. Sometimes, simply seeing all your options written out plainly can help you discern where God may be leading you next.

Janis's Story

When my son was diagnosed with autism at three years old, we were encouraged to enroll him in an early intervention program.

We had two options. Either I could enroll him in a half-day program three days a week, or I could enroll him in a full-day inclusion program five days a week.

Although I was used to having my son home with me all day, it was clear that the full-day option was the best choice for our family. While the half-day program was more convenient and allowed my son to stay home more, the full-day program would be better suited to meet his needs.

I prayed that God would either open a door wide open or slam it in my face, and He's always been clear when it comes to my son's needs. We decided to enroll my son in the full-day option, despite judgmental comments from friends and family who didn't support what God was leading us to do.

Now my son is entering fifth grade this year. He's attended a mainstream school since kindergarten, and most people find it hard to believe that he even has autism. He's come so far, and it was all due to his early intervention.

I'm so thankful we obeyed God's prompting even though it was difficult at the time.

6. Have Trusted Mentors Affirmed This Decision?

In her book *Fervent*, well-known author and speaker Priscilla Shirer shares how she received confirmation of God's will for her life while attending a local Bible study:

> The person who was teaching from the Bible that day—a man I'd never met beforehand, a man who didn't know me or anything about me—looked my direction and spoke directly to me.... I held my breath while he told me in vivid terms that, among other things, he sensed I would have the privilege of calling many people to prayer during my lifetime. And not just to prayer but to a refreshed, renewed focus and fervency of prayer they'd never known before.[16]

What an amazing experience! However, for most of us, discerning God's will for our lives is rarely so easy. Instead of one miraculous sign, we typically have to follow several smaller clues and then ask godly friends, family, or mentors, "Am I hearing this right? Could this be God's will for my life?"

Thankfully, God often gives us godly friends and mentors for exactly this reason—to let us know when we're way off base, to reassure us when we're on the right track, and to warn us of any potential blind spots or wrong turns we might otherwise miss.

This doesn't mean your friends and family will always understand or support your goals and dreams, however. It's normal for those who care about us to have questions, concerns, and fears, and sadly, some people may never fully be on board with God's plan for your life.

In fact, some may even try to dissuade you from following God's will—either out of their own pride and selfishness or because they heard God wrong themselves.

This happened to me at a Christian women's conference a few years ago.

A woman I had never met before gave me stern advice that she was convinced was God's will for my life. She insisted that I was living in fear and I needed to trust God (and follow her advice), no matter what problems it could cause.

While I certainly believe God can speak to us through others, and I didn't disagree with her logic, her advice truly didn't make sense for my situation for a number of reasons. Thankfully, I consulted with multiple godly friends and family members (who do know me well), and they confirmed that I was right not to follow her advice.

This is why it's so important to seek wisdom, perspective, and advice from several Christian friends and mentors who know you well and whose advice you can trust. Not everyone will always agree with you, but God often uses friends, family, and mentors to help guide our decision-making.

Dive Deeper into Scripture

→ Read 1 Timothy 4:11–16. How did Paul affirm Timothy's gifting? How did Paul encourage Timothy to provide this same mentorship and guidance to others?

→ Read Proverbs 11:14; 12:15; 15:22. Why is it so important
to seek the wisdom and advice of multiple friends,
family members, and mentors?

Brenna's Story

Though I was raised Catholic, my family never discussed abortion. As a young girl, I only vaguely knew that it was something that hurt babies. Yet even at that young age, I felt so strongly that it was wrong that I wore a baby feet pin on the lapel of my school uniform.

In high school, I still didn't exactly know what abortion was. But when the faculty moderator of our school's Respect Life Club saw my fire for the cause, she let me borrow her copy of *Unplanned*—the story of Abby Johnson's conversion from Planned Parenthood director to pro-life advocate.

From that moment, I knew my calling. I knew I was called to be part of the pro-life movement until all of God's children were equally valued by our society. I went on to lead the Students for Life group at my university before being hired to work for Students for Life of America. Now I get to write for the best pro-life organization in America.

I'm all in on the fight against abortion. And quite frankly, I couldn't have assembled a better career for myself. There's no doubt it's been divinely handcrafted, and I'm infinitely grateful.

7. Is There a Way to Test the Waters?

If, after going through each of these questions, you're still unsure about which direction to take, the best way to find additional clarity is often by trying new opportunities and seeing where they lead.

Sign up for a club. Take a class. Volunteer in an area you want to learn more about. Shadow a friend at a job you're considering. Interview an expert on a subject you're interested in. Read books. Listen to podcasts. Watch documentaries. Sign up for a short-term mission trip.

If you fall in love with an experience, you can take the next steps from there. If not, you can try something else, but at least you will have learned something along the way.

Clarity often results from action, not the other way around.

Part 2

Follow God's Will

7

Cultivating Spiritual Disciplines

*How do I live out my faith
on a day-to-day basis?*

I love my children. I really do. But sometimes they drive me bananas.

At the time of this writing, one of my children has a habit of stashing their dirty underwear behind the bathroom sink, one consistently takes fifteen minutes to pull their socks on, and one regularly leaves a trail of toys and half-eaten snacks wherever they go.

Every single day, I find myself saying things like "Please take your plate to the sink before the puppy gets it." "Stop chasing your brother through the house." "Put the broom down before you break something." "Don't even *think* about bringing those muddy shoes inside this house." "Are you *trying* to drive me crazy??"

Yes. Yes, they are. In fact, the other night at bedtime, one of my adorable little children prayed, "Dear God, please help me drive my mom *nuts*!" before bursting into giggles.

Whether you have young children at home, aging parents, serious health concerns, a demanding job, or anything else that makes your life feel chaotic at times, it can certainly be easy to wish your life were a bit simpler, calmer, or less stressful.

After all, surely your faith would be stronger if your life were easier, right? Just think of how much time you could spend in the Word if you weren't constantly putting out fires every day.

As nice as this sounds, it reminds me of a sermon I heard several years ago.

Throughout the book of Exodus, we read incredible stories of Moses standing up to Pharaoh, delivering God's people from Egypt, drawing water from a rock, and spending months with God on Mount Sinai, where he received the Ten Commandments.

As incredible as these experiences would have been, however, Moses couldn't stay on the literal or metaphorical mountaintop with God forever. Moses needed to come down off the mountain and lead the people according to God's direction. He needed to teach the Israelites to obey God's commands and oversee the work God had asked them to do.

The pastor who preached this sermon shared, "Everyone wants to have these incredible mountaintop experiences with God, and sometimes we do. But we can't live our whole lives on the mountain. Real faith is lived out in the valleys."

I love mountaintop experiences. I think we all do. Yet our call as Christians isn't to set up camp at the top of the spiritual "mountain"—far away from all the people and pressures of the world—where we can seek God and worship Him without interruption.

Instead, for most of us, God calls us to serve Him in the midst of our busy day-to-day lives as we learn to love our families, care for our neighbors, and do our jobs well.

The valley is where real faith is grown, tested, and refined. The valley shapes our character and provides us countless opportunities to live out God's commands and share God's light with others.

That's why, in this chapter, we want to explore the question, How do we live out our Christian faith on an ordinary, day-to-day level? What does it look like to follow God's will *in between* the mountaintop experiences, when we aren't actively pursuing God's purpose for our entire lives?

What does it look like to follow Jesus on a random Tuesday morning, Thursday night, or Saturday afternoon? How can we follow God's will right where we are today?

Dive Deeper into Scripture

→ Read Exodus 19:1–8. Approximately how long had it been since God brought the Israelites out of Egypt? What promise did God make to the people? What promise did the people make?

→ Read Exodus 24:15–18; 32:1–4. How long was Moses on the mountain with God? What happened while he was gone?

→ Read Exodus 32:19–28, 33–35, and try to picture the scene. Why couldn't Moses stay on the mountaintop with God? Why couldn't Moses stay solely in the valley?

Carmen's Story

I start by praying and talking to God in the morning.... I ask to be a good wife, mother, daughter, sister, and friend. All day I talk to Him, asking for guidance in all that I do. You do your best every day and just know that it gets easier every day with practice.

Practicing Spiritual Disciplines

One of the easiest ways to grow your faith on a daily basis is to practice various spiritual disciplines. If you aren't familiar with the term, spiritual disciplines are small habits or practices you can do to strengthen your faith and your relationship with God. Common examples include:

- prayer
- Bible study
- Scripture memorization
- self-reflection
- Sabbath rest
- fellowship
- solitude
- stewardship

The Bible never tells us how often, how long, or to what extent we should practice each of these spiritual disciplines. Rather, the Bible simply encourages us to incorporate as many of these practices as we can, as we have the time, opportunity, and desire to do so.

For this reason, the way you practice these spiritual disciplines will likely look different than the way your friends, family, or other Christians you know practice them. And it's both common and healthy for your spiritual practices to change over time, especially when you enter a new season.

To give a personal example, fifteen years ago, when I was healing from the spiritual warfare, depression, and eating disorder I dealt with throughout high school and college, I went through a period marked by solitude, self-reflection, and prayer. I didn't participate in fellowship, I wasn't out sharing the gospel, and I certainly didn't fast.

Ten years ago, when I was a young stay-at-home mom with little ones, my focus shifted to discipling my children, serving my local church, volunteering in my community, and being a good steward of my time, talent, and resources.

Today my life looks radically different than it did fifteen, ten, or even five years ago.

These days, I spend more time studying and teaching God's Word than ever before. I'm currently able to mentor and evangelize on a much greater scale than I have in the past (which is wonderful!), but this means I've also had to be very intentional about observing Sabbath rest, silence, and prayer. As a result, I don't get to worship, fellowship, or volunteer nearly as often as I'd like.

I do want to spend more time on each of these disciplines in the future, but I'm only one person, and I can't possibly do everything all at once (no matter how much I try).

This is what makes sense for me and my life right now. So how about you? Which spiritual disciplines would you most benefit from in your current season? Let's look at each a bit more in-depth below to help you decide.

Lucy's Story

I get up early before my family wakes up and give the day to God. I read through the Bible in One Year app,[1] give thanks, and try to start each day by being positive.

Prayer

Of all the spiritual disciplines, prayer is arguably the easiest practice to begin. Prayer requires no preplanning, no materials, and very little time. You can pray absolutely anywhere, at any time, for any length of time—including taking a second to say a quick prayer right now!

For many people, the easiest way to get started with prayer is simply by talking to God as they go throughout their day. In fact, 1 Thessalonians 5:17 encourages us to do this when it instructs us to "pray continually."

Yes, it can be extremely valuable to set aside time specifically for prayer—whether at church, on a retreat, or at home—but there's no need to wait until you can find a quiet spot where you won't be interrupted. Depending on your current season of life, that may not be realistic for you right now.

Instead, start a running conversation with God as you go about your day, the same way you might chat with a friend who stopped by for a surprise visit. You can do this either out loud or in your head—whichever is most comfortable for you.

Not sure what to pray? There are several prayer formulas you can use if you'd like a little more structure. Personally, I was taught the ACTS method, and I still use it to this day.

ACTS stands for adoration, confession, thanksgiving, and supplication.

1. **A—Adoration:** Praise God for how good and wonderful He is, acknowledging specific ways He has come through in your life or specific attributes of His you admire.

2. **C—Confession:** Admit your sins to God and ask for His forgiveness.

3. **T—Thanksgiving:** Thank God for everything He has done for you, in you, and through you (and others).

4. **S—Supplication:** Ask God to supply whatever you need.

This is just one method, of course.

You could pray a prewritten prayer such as the Lord's Prayer (the Our Father),[2] the Glory Be,[3] or the Magnificat,[4] each of which can easily be found online. You could pray through the Scriptures—for example, by reciting psalms (or any other passages of Scripture you relate to) as heartfelt prayers to God.

Or you could follow the Lectio Divina prayer style. Dating back to AD 330, this spiritual practice, which combines both Scripture and prayer, was originally designed to help early Christian monks meditate more deeply on God's Word in prayer.[5]

Lectio Divina also consists of four steps. Here's how to pray in this style if you'd like to give it a try:

1. **Lectio (Read):** Read a Bible passage slowly, paying attention to small details in the text. Are there any words or thoughts that jump out at you? Don't be afraid to linger over the text.

2. **Meditatio (Reflect):** Read through the passage a second time, prayerfully reflecting on the text. Notice any thoughts or feelings that arise. Do you sense God speaking anything to you as you meditate on His Word?

3. **Oratio (Respond):** As you continue to meditate on the text, offer any thoughts, feelings, or requests up to God, and then listen for His response. Many people find it helpful to journal their thoughts at this point.

4. **Contemplatio (Rest):** Finally, spend a few minutes in quiet contemplation, leaving room for God to speak to you through His Word or through the Holy Spirit.

Altogether, the Lectio Divina process may take twenty to thirty minutes.

Don't worry if you can't always spare long stretches of time for quiet prayer, however. While dedicated time in prayer is certainly beneficial, it's completely normal for the majority of your prayers to be short conversations with God as you go about your daily routine.

Your prayers do not have to be long and complicated, and it's okay if you're not sure exactly what to say. In fact, Romans 8:26 assures us, "The Spirit helps us in our weakness. We do not know what we ought to pray for, but the Spirit himself intercedes for us through wordless groans."

Think of prayer as simply a conversation with the God who loves you very much and who wants to have a close, meaningful relationship with you.

Dive Deeper into Scripture

→ Read Matthew 6:9–13. What does Jesus pray for in this passage? Are we required to say these exact same words when we pray? Why might we choose to?

→ Read Matthew 5:44; 26:41; Ephesians 6:18; Philippians 4:6; I Timothy 2:1–2; and James 5:13. According to these verses, what types of things can we pray for?

Sara's Story

One way I live out my faith is through consistent prayer. I say a morning offering each day as I wake up. We pray before meals. I pray with my husband. And I have a prayer board above the coffeepot, where my adult children can put up sticky notes with their prayer requests.

I attend daily mass on my days off work, as well as on Saturdays. I meet with a friend weekly to go over readings and commentary from a book we are reading. I also post about saints, mass times, and seasonal church events on my Facebook profile.

Bible Study

In *Fall in Love with God's Word*, I share at length about how to create a personal Bible reading routine you will love.

The chapter about creating a quiet time plan (chapter 4) is especially helpful if you want to read your Bible more often but you struggle to find time to read it consistently.

Here's the condensed version: Start by considering your current season and personal preferences. Then use this information to answer the following questions and create your quiet time plan.

- When will you read your Bible?
- Where will you read your Bible?
- How often will you read your Bible?
- How long will you spend in God's Word?
- What else will you do during your quiet time?

Once you have the first draft of your quiet time plan, put it into practice for about a week, and then evaluate. Which parts are working or not working? If you're having trouble sticking to your original plan, what specific detail is throwing you offtrack?

If you consistently struggle to read God's Word regularly, the problem isn't you. It's your plan. Don't fall for the lie that you can't do it, you're a failure, or you're just not motivated enough. These are lies and distractions. Instead, simply tweak your plan as needed until you figure out what works best for you in this season, knowing that your plan will likely change and adapt over time.

If this is an area you'd like to grow in, you can find *Fall in Love with God's Word: Practical Strategies for Busy Women*, along with a growing collection of free printable resources—all designed to help you create a quiet time you love—by visiting FallinLovewithGodsWord.com.

Alternately, if you already read your Bible regularly and you're looking to take your study even deeper, the *Follow God's Will* companion workbook has plenty of additional information, exercises, and printables to help you get the most out of your time in God's Word. You can find it at EquippingGodlyWomen.com/Follow-Gods-Will.

Scripture Memorization

Scripture memorization is a great way to make sure you always have God's Word with you whenever and wherever you need it. Plus, it's easier and more enjoyable than you might think.

For example, common ways to memorize Scripture include writing verses on a mirror, on notecards, or on jewelry you'll see often, putting verses to music, or simply repeating the verses out loud again and again until they're familiar.

When I help my children memorize Bible passages, I'll typically write the verses on a small dry-erase board and have my kids read them out loud multiple times, removing a word or two each time, until they can say the whole thing by memory.

Don't be afraid to get creative and have fun with it! The more Scripture you know, the more wisdom and encouragement you'll have readily available to you.

Dive Deeper into Scripture

→ Read Joshua 1:7–8. What instruction does the Lord give Joshua in this passage? Why does the Lord give Joshua this instruction? How might this passage apply to us today? (Think: main idea.)

→ Read Psalm 119:9–16. How does this unnamed psalmist feel about God's Word? Notice the verbs in this passage. What does this psalmist do and not do?

Sidnee's Story

One way I live out my faith on a day-to-day basis is by learning to rely on prayer to get through the tough moments. I'm also having fun introducing my one- and two-year-old toddlers to the lives of the saints.

Self-Reflection

Self-reflection is the practice of intentionally thinking about your life and evaluating it in terms of where you are and where you'd like to be. There are several ways to do this.

You can read your Bible slowly, examining and comparing yourself against the standards set forth in Scripture. You can do the same with Christian-living books, biographies, and Bible studies (as long as you are careful to make sure the examples and advice they share are in line with God's Word).

You can also train yourself to pay attention to your actions and reactions throughout the day, asking yourself questions such as:

- What does the way I spend my time and money say about my priorities?
- Where am I falling short of God's will for my life?
- What specific obstacles are preventing me from following God's will for my life?
- What small steps can I take today to live out my faith more fully tomorrow?

Questions like these can provide valuable insights into both your strengths and your weaknesses as a Christian woman, wife, mother, sister, coworker, or friend.

From there, you can pray and ask the Holy Spirit for strength to live out your calling well. And don't hesitate to intentionally seek out additional resources (books, classes, mentors, etc.) to make progress in any areas where you might be struggling.

As beautifully imperfect human beings, we'll never achieve perfection on this side of heaven, but God does promise to help us grow and mature in our faith and in our callings, through the help of the Holy Spirit, if we ask.

Dive Deeper into Scripture

→ Read Lamentations 3:40–42; 1 John 1:9; and 1 Corinthians 11:28–32. Why should we examine

ourselves, according to these passages? What is likely
to happen if we don't?

→ Read Matthew 7:3–5. Does this passage say
we can *never* judge others? What do we need
to do first? Why? What might happen if we
don't?

Sabbath Rest

In today's busy culture, finding time for Sabbath rest isn't always
easy, but that doesn't mean it isn't important. In fact, I'd argue that
many of us *need* God's gift of Sabbath rest more than ever. (I know
I do!)

Sure, you may not be able to spend your entire Sunday lounging
around in quiet worship, but what *can* you do to slow down and
receive God's rest?

Could you clean the house, run errands, and meal plan earlier in
the week so you can set Sunday aside as a day of worship? Alternately,
could you look for ways to add fun, restful, or rejuvenating activities
into your day?

This past Sabbath I read a good book, went for a six-mile run,
and snuggled up to watch a movie with my kids. My husband slept
in, watched football, did a little yardwork, and took our kids for a
walk. And of course, our whole family went to church.

We still made lunch and dinner. My husband cleaned up after
lunch, and I folded a load of laundry. But overall, it was a very relaxing, enjoyable day.

How can you create the same for your family?

Dive Deeper into Scripture

→ Read Exodus 20:8–11; Ezekiel 20:19–20; and Hebrews 4:9–11. Why did God require the Israelites to practice the Sabbath? Why does He give us a Sabbath today? How might our lives be different if we committed to practicing Sabbath?

→ Read Mark 2:23–28 and Luke 13:10–17. Why were the religious leaders so offended by Jesus and His disciples' actions? How did Jesus explain their behavior? What main idea can we glean from these passages?

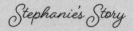

Stephanie's Story

As a Catholic Christian, I live out my faith by going to mass on Sundays and by keeping the Sabbath. I also abstain [from meat] on Fridays and pray every time I pass a cemetery, funeral procession, or accident.

Fellowship

Are you regularly spending time with other believers who encourage you, inspire you, challenge you, and hold you accountable? If not, you're missing out!

You can connect with other like-minded Christians by getting involved in Sunday school classes, Bible studies, or volunteer opportunities available through your church. You can reach out to friends, family, and coworkers you already know. Or you can find online communities, including Christian Facebook groups, chat rooms, and forums.

For example, if you're looking for mentorship, friendship, and accountability in the form of an online coaching group for Christian women, we'd love to have you check out the Equipping Godly Women membership community. You can learn more at EquippingGodlyWomen.com/membership.

Dive Deeper into Scripture

→ Read Hebrews 10:23–25 and I Thessalonians 5:II. What does Paul urge the believers to do in these passages? Why does Paul encourage this behavior?

→ Read James 5:16; Galatians 6:I; and I John I:8–10. Why is it important for us to confess our sins to one another? What might happen if we do? What might happen if we don't?

Solitude

Do you ever feel as though you're so busy taking care of everyone and everything else that you barely have time to think, much less spend time in prayer and reading God's Word?

As busy Christian women, it can be difficult to find time for solitude. But it's still important to carve out space to think, process, and pray.

When can you find time to yourself? Can you wake up fifteen minutes earlier or stay up fifteen minutes later? Can you sneak away to a quiet spot for half an hour during naptime, during your lunch break, or while the kids are watching cartoons? Would your husband be willing to take over the bedtime routine so you have time to yourself? Can you trade babysitting with another mom in your area?

Two years ago, I started taking short walks around my neighborhood whenever I could spare a few minutes. Eventually this led to long-distance running, where I can be alone with my thoughts for hours at a time. Obviously, this isn't something I can do every day, and it may not be the right solution for you, but what *can* you do?

Dive Deeper into Scripture

→ Read Mark 1:32–35 and Luke 5:12–16. How did Jesus find time for solitude? What did He give up to find this time? What does this tell us about our ability to find time for solitude today?

Sue's Story

One way I live out my faith on a day-to-day basis is by reading my devotional every day. I also grab my Bible when I have a few minutes.

When I'm not able to sit and read, I talk to God in my mind all day long. It keeps me close to Him and helps me focus on the positive things in my life.

Stewardship

If you aren't familiar with the term *stewardship*, it means managing your time, talent, and resources wisely so you can provide for yourself, your family, and others in need.

We see it in 1 Peter 4:10, which says, "Each of you should use whatever gift you have received to serve others, as faithful stewards of God's grace in its various forms."

So what skills, resources, or abilities has God blessed you with? How can you use them to bless others?

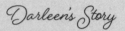

Darleen's Story

I'm human and fail on a day-to-day basis. However, each day I take time to think about what I'd like to do for the day, set my mental attitude, and go for it. I also take time to pray for guidance and give thanks.

Can you cook a meal, organize a fundraiser, run a social media account, decorate a nursery, run errands, or provide fun after-school activities for kids in your neighborhood? Can you donate time, money, canned goods, clothes, or household items to churches, schools, or nonprofits in your area?

God doesn't bless us with extra so we can keep it for ourselves. He blesses us with more than we need so we can then turn around and be a blessing to others. Opportunities are all around us every day. We simply need to keep our eyes open for opportunities to serve!

Dive Deeper into Scripture

→ Read 1 Timothy 6:17–19 and 2 Corinthians 9:6–8. What does God call us to do with our excess? Why is this important?

→ Read Colossians 3:18–24. What does the phrase
   "as working for the Lord" (v. 23) mean? Why
   should we work in this way? What benefit will
   we see?

Avoid the Checklist Mentality

Hopefully, reading this chapter has inspired you to try a few new spiritual disciplines while continuing your current ones. As you do, however, I want to caution you against what I call "the checklist mentality."

Our goal as Christians isn't to get as many spiritual checkmarks as possible in an attempt to make God happy or to earn our good standing. It's to love God and others well.

If you missed church because you were caring for a sick toddler, that's okay. If you missed your prayer time because your husband or teenager needed to talk, that's okay too. If you didn't read your Bible because you were busy helping a neighbor in need, that's perfectly fine.

Yes, spiritual disciplines are important. We should pursue them in order to grow in our faith. But we must always remember that spiritual disciplines are meant to help us live out our primary call to love God and others, *not* to replace it.

This is why, in the parable of the good Samaritan,[6] Jesus commends the Samaritan man who took time out of his day to help someone in need, but does not commend the Levite and the priest who hurried past, likely on their way to or from worship at the temple.

Yes, we should practice our spiritual disciplines (prayer, Bible study, regular church attendance, etc.), but we also need to make sure we're finding real opportunities to put the Christian principles we're learning into practice.

We can't spend so much time in prayer or Bible study that we neglect the real needs of those around us, nor can we spend so much time with those around us that we completely neglect our own relationship with God either. There has to be a balance.

8

Standing Strong for What You Believe

How do I live out my faith when others disagree?

"Do you have time to talk? I need advice. How do I stop being such a people pleaser?"

She was laughing, but underneath the laughter, I could sense a real internal struggle. She wanted to make what she knew was the right decision for her family, but not everyone in her life agreed. And even though she had politely explained her reasoning, the pressure to give in to their demands was strong.

Have you ever felt this way?

You want to be a strong, committed Christian who boldly lives out your faith on a day-to-day basis, but it's hard when you don't have your friends' and family's support.

Maybe you've gotten clear pushback. Others have told you in no uncertain terms that you aren't allowed, you shouldn't, or you can't. Maybe they've told you, "Be smart" or "Don't get too carried away."

Or perhaps the pressure is more subtle. No one has said anything (yet), but their sighs and glances make their feelings clear.

Either way, you're worried that if you go *all in* with your faith, your friends and family may start pulling away. You don't want to be seen as weird, intolerant, closed-minded, or hypocritical, so you've been quietly shying away from expressing what you truly think, feel, or want.

It isn't just you.

There have been plenty of times when I didn't speak up, when I went along with things I didn't agree with, or when I didn't share the dreams God had placed on my heart for fear of being criticized or rejected. It happens to all of us at one time or another.

That's why, in this chapter, we're discussing seven practical ways we can stand strong in our faith and do what we know is right—even when those around us don't understand or agree.

Andreana's Story

As a sixteen-year-old, I have always called myself a Christian, but I never truly lived for Christ. Instead, I spent years afraid to show and express my faith.

I remember sitting with my friends in church when I was twelve or thirteen. I wanted to sing the songs, but I felt stuck. My palms were sweaty, my heart was pounding, and I couldn't sing a lyric. I would just sing in my heart and whisper the songs. This went on for years!

Thankfully, this last year has completely changed my walk with Christ.

While I do still struggle from time to time, I am no longer afraid to live out my faith. My lukewarm friends and family do not hold me back in any way.

Recently, I watched a video about being bold in the Lord. The next day, I woke up early and wrote six letters full of verses and encouragement about how much Jesus loves and accepts us just as we are. I went to six of my neighbors' houses and left the gospel of their salvation, then ran all the way home!

As a minor, there are still some things I can't do, but I try to live out my faith as much as I can. It took a really long time to get to where I am now, but I just give all the glory to God that I'm here now!

How to Prioritize God When Friends and Family Disagree

So how can we live out our faith boldly and unapologetically, particularly when those around us disagree? When should we stay quiet to keep the peace, and when should we stand up for what we know is right?

Here are seven practical steps to help you stand strong and do what's right, even when you face opposition.

I. Surround Yourself with Christian Community

I've always loved the Jim Rohn quote, "You are the average of the five people you spend the most time with."[1] It's the same advice we see in 1 Corinthians 15:33: "Do not be misled: 'Bad company corrupts good character.'"

So who are the five people you spend the most time around? What do they value? What do they prioritize? Are they pursuing God wholeheartedly, or do they call themselves Christians while living lifestyles that don't match what they say they believe?

Please don't misunderstand me here. If your closest friends and family are lukewarm, atheist, or agnostic, this doesn't mean you need to cut them out of your life. Those relationships are important as well, and we'll discuss them more in-depth in the next chapter.

However, it does mean you may need to cultivate some new friendships with people outside of your current circle. This way, you'll have a solid support system to help you stand strong when living out your faith isn't always easy.

Do you want to be a supportive wife who refuses to speak poorly of your husband when he isn't around? Do you want to be a patient, involved mom? Do you want to be an overseas missionary, a successful Christian business owner, or simply a Christian who is passionate about living out your faith to the best of your ability every day? If so, it helps to surround yourself with other believers who are pursuing similar goals.

You can often find these new friendships through church, school, Bible studies, volunteer opportunities, and other activities or clubs you may belong to. You can also seek out Christian friends and mentors online—through blogs, Facebook groups, podcasts, and forums.

And don't forget, we have an awesome membership community of wonderful, Jesus-loving women at Equipping Godly Women, where you can get the advice, encouragement, and support you need. You can learn more at EquippingGodlyWomen.com/membership.

Dive Deeper into Scripture

→ Read Proverbs 13:20. In what ways have you seen this principle play out in your own life or in the lives of those around you?

→ Read 1 Timothy 4:12 and Titus 2:1–7a. What are a few practical ways your friendship could encourage or inspire those around you? How have other believers encouraged or inspired you in your faith?

2. Know What You Believe and Why

Whether your friends, family, or coworkers are skeptical of Christianity or they're merely curious about the positive changes they've seen in your life lately, if you're living out your faith boldly enough, it's highly likely that someone will ask you questions about what you believe and why.

When this happens, will you have a clear answer? Or will you miss an opportunity to share your faith because you're not really sure what you believe, why you believe it, and where to find the answer in Scripture?

Now, to be clear, you don't have to know the answer to *every* question. It's okay to say, "That's a great question! Let me do a little research and get back to you on that." But if there are specific issues you know you are likely to be questioned on, it can be very helpful to do a bit of research in advance.

My previous book, *Fall in Love with God's Word*, has an entire chapter on how to study Scripture for answers to common questions. Alternately, you can visit your local Christian bookstore or public library for fantastic books on various topics. Or you can read online articles, listen to podcasts, or make an appointment to speak with your pastor or priest.

There are so many fantastic resources available to you if you're willing to seek them out. Not only will these resources allow you to witness to others, but they're sure to strengthen your own faith as well.

Dive Deeper into Scripture

→ Read 1 Peter 3:15–16 and Colossians 4:5–6. In addition to being prepared to give an answer, what other command do both of these passages give us? Why is this so important?

→ Read 2 Timothy 4:2–5. How do we see this passage reflected in our current culture? What is our responsibility as believers? What do we need to do in advance so we can better live out the commands in verse 2?

Paulette's Story

As a Jew for Jesus, I have felt so much pressure to hide my relationship with the Lord God Almighty. When I first got saved thirty-five years ago, all I did was talk about my new relationship with Jesus/Yeshua. Unfortunately, this turned a lot of people off.

My family thinks I'm a traitor to my Jewish roots. I tried explaining that Jesus was a Jew, but it doesn't matter. They don't want to hear about what I believe. They're completely closed off to anything about Jesus.

I've been praying for my family for thirty years, and I'm still praying today that the Jewish people would learn who their Messiah is. I try not to push my beliefs on anyone, but just live out my faith. If they see something about me that they like, I am open to sharing.

Instead, I share the Lord Jesus with strangers wherever I go. I have never stopped talking about Him, and as a result, I have brought many people to the Lord.

3. Make Pleasing God Your Number-One Priority

Often one of the most difficult aspects of standing strong in your faith is knowing that it may lead to others' disapproval. As human beings, we are hardwired to want the approval and acceptance of others. And yet we must remember that our ultimate goal in life isn't to make other people like us but to love God and others and to live out His call for us.

Sometimes God's call on our lives will be to share the gospel boldly so that others can come to faith too. Other times He may simply ask us to set forth a quiet example of what following Christ can look like. Both are important ways of sharing the same gospel message and glorifying God.

Either way, we must remember this: It isn't our job to try to "save" anyone or convince others to think or behave the same way we do. Rather, as Christians, we should be prepared simply to share what we know, believe, and have experienced so that others can respond if and when the Holy Spirit prompts them and they decide they are ready.

Thankfully, this takes a lot of pressure off. No longer do you have to worry about persuading people and repelling them. Instead, you can naturally share within your relationships and let people decide on their own.

Now, to be clear, there's nothing wrong with wanting to be liked. We were created to live in community, and we should strive to live at peace and enjoy deeply fulfilling relationships. But we must remember that these relationships aren't our ultimate goal.

Someday we will stand before God to give an account of how we used the one and only life He gave us. May we never say, "Sorry, I completely failed the mission You gave me. I was too worried about what my friends and family might think."

So ask yourself, *Is my primary aim really to love God and love others, or am I more concerned with what other people think?*

Dive Deeper into Scripture

→ Read Exodus 20:1–6; I Kings 14:22; and 2 Corinthians 11:2–3. In what way is God jealous? Is it sinful for God to be jealous? How is godly jealousy different

STANDING STRONG FOR WHAT YOU BELIEVE   147

than human jealousy (which the Bible warns against
elsewhere)?

→ Read Matthew 10:32–39. What is the main idea of this
passage? What practical implications does it have for
our lives today?

4. Determine Your Actions in Advance

Are there any cultural, political, or ethical issues you already know
you and your friends or family disagree on? For example, maybe your
views differ on current political issues, specific health care mandates,
popular lifestyle choices, or which types of media or topics of conversation are appropriate.

How will you respond if your friends or family ask, insist, or
expect you to behave in a way that is contrary to your religious beliefs
and convictions?

While it's impossible to foresee every potential disagreement you
might have with friends and family, if you know certain topics are
likely to be an issue, it's wise to make decisions in advance when
you're more likely to think rationally rather than waiting until you
are in the midst of an uncomfortable situation.

You can't control the choices or reactions of others; every person
is entitled to make their own decisions—whether right or wrong.
But you have a choice in how *you* will respond.

So decide in advance. What will you do or not do? Where do you
draw the line? How are your friends and family likely to respond,
and how will you deal with that? What will you tell yourself when
you're tempted to back down or give in? Then be prepared to follow
through even when it isn't easy, convenient, or socially acceptable.

Dive Deeper into Scripture

→ Read Joshua 24:14–22. Why did Joshua ask the people to officially reaffirm their commitment to follow God? What was at stake if they disobeyed?

→ Read I Peter 5:8 and I Corinthians 10:13. How can deciding our actions in advance help us avoid sin? What specific advantages will we have?

Crystal's Story

When I was younger, I used to feel pressured to let things slide and not stand up for myself or my faith because I wasn't confident enough to support my view.

I didn't want to lose a friend because of our differences in how we saw the world and the part we play in it. And I thought, *Who am I to judge?* After all, I was a sinner too. I didn't realize how important it was to be the light and show an example of a faith-filled life.

I don't know if my actions or lack thereof have impacted anyone in a positive or negative way, but I hope that people see Christ in me.

5. Help Your Friends and Family Understand Any New Changes They See

Last night, after the kids went to bed, my husband and I had a heart-to-heart. With plenty of grace and love, he asked me about a few of my recent choices and what they meant for the future of our family.

"Are things changing?" he asked. "That's fine if they are, but I'd like to know. We should talk about it."

The truth is, I *have* been acting a bit different lately, but not for any of the negative reasons he may have feared. Our family is simply in a period of transition right now, and it was good for us to sit down and have that conversation.

Thankfully, our conversation went really well. He shared his concerns, we talked things through, and we were able to find a great solution that works for both of us.

Unfortunately, not all friends and family respond so well to change.

This is why it can be helpful to sit down and discuss any changes you'd like to make in advance, rather than waiting until you find yourself in the midst of an awkward situation.

Do you want to wake up early to spend time in God's Word? Do you want to switch churches, give more generously to those in need, or sign up for a new volunteer opportunity? Do you need to stop watching certain TV shows or stop listening to certain types of music?

If so, you may want to let your friends and family know in advance. This will allow you the opportunity to answer any questions they may have and to take their thoughts and preferences into consideration as well—especially if the decision you want to make affects your entire family. While you shouldn't use others' preferences as an excuse to prevent you from wholeheartedly following God, by discussing the wants and expectations of others openly and honestly in advance, you can avoid disagreements and hurt feelings later on.

Dive Deeper into Scripture

→ Read I Corinthians 9:19–23. How did Paul express his faith differently, depending on his audience? Why did he do this? Does this passage encourage us to participate in sin in an attempt to increase our witness?

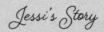

Jessi's Story

When I married my husband, he was an atheist who was very against tithing.

Growing up in an extremely impoverished neighborhood just a few miles from a megachurch full of wealthy people who passed out Bibles but did nothing to help their financial situation, he felt that all the church wanted was money. After all, where were they for his best friend's family after he was gunned down only seven houses from his own? As a result, he was very angry and didn't trust the church—any church—with money.

Even after my husband eventually became a baptized believer, it took several years for him to be okay with giving money to the church.

For many of those years, fellow Christians told me how wrong I was for not tithing and that I should go behind my husband's back and tithe because "it's in the Bible" and we were "going to hell for not obeying God."

However, I spent many hours in prayer and adoration, and God's promise to me was that one day we'd be able to tithe—that my husband's heart would soften, and he would come around. I just needed to be patient.

Honoring my husband's wishes was extremely hard—especially in a world that tells women we don't need a man and that we can do what we want. It was incredibly hard to stay focused on God's voice when so many other voices around me were telling me how wrong I was.

But now I'm able to tithe, and I am married to a man who loves Jesus, all because I listened to His voice and not the ones around me.

6. Pray for Courage

One of my favorite passages of the entire Bible is found in Acts 4.

In the previous chapter, Peter and John cause quite the public spectacle—healing a crippled beggar and preaching boldly in a public square, leading hundreds (if not thousands) of people to Christ.

Not surprisingly, this infuriates the local religious leaders, who throw the two men in jail before threatening them and commanding them to stop preaching in Jesus' name.

With their lives at stake, you might expect the apostles to shrink back in fear, but this isn't what we see next. Instead, the apostles pray, "Now, Lord, consider their threats and enable your servants to speak your word with great boldness" (Acts 4:29).

What an incredible prayer! And the Bible says God answered their prayer.

Can you imagine if government officials began threatening, beating, imprisoning, and murdering Christians? Would you shrink back in silence, or would you continue to boldly proclaim God's name, knowing that you or your family could be brutally tortured or killed as a result? Most of us won't share the gospel for fear of being embarrassed or uncomfortable—much less murdered.

Yet the same God who granted the apostles' prayer for boldness two thousand years ago still answers our prayers today. Ask God for His strength, conviction, and protection, trusting that He will provide you with everything you need.

Dive Deeper into Scripture

→ Read Acts 4:23–24, 29–31. How does God answer the apostles' prayers in this passage? What types of prayers might you pray if you knew for certain God would answer them?

→ Read Joshua 1:1–9. What promises do we see the Lord give Joshua in this passage? What command do we see God repeat three times? What would allow Joshua to live out this difficult command?

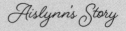

Aislynn's Story

I have several non-Christian family members and friends. I have felt pressured to not speak about my faith, reference Scripture, or share sermons with them because it makes them feel uncomfortable.

With several non-Christian friends, my sharing of my faith has caused us to no longer be close, leaving our friendships superficial and shallow.

Though I am growing stronger and more vocal about my faith in Christ since coming back to Jesus, these situations are not easy for me. I frequently worry about what others think because I don't want to cause them to distrust me or view me as hypocritical because of my previous waywardness.

Despite this, I know that only God can change their hearts. I continue to pray and am not giving up hope that they will eventually turn toward the cross.

7. Start Small

A few years ago, I attended a conference where we were asked to choose two words: one that would no longer define us and one that would. I don't remember the word I chose to get rid of, but I do remember the one I wanted to keep. I wrote the word *brave* in nice, neat letters on a small gray rock. Then I brought the rock home and put it on my shelf, where I'd see it often.

After all, I had big dreams I felt God was calling me to accomplish (I still do!), and I knew I would have to be brave if I wanted to live them out.

Ever since the day I brought that rock home, do you know what changed?

Absolutely nothing. Not a single thing. In fact, I completely forgot the rock was there.

You see, it isn't enough to simply wish or hope you'll be brave enough to live out God's call on your life when the time comes. You have to actually take action.

So why not start today? Rather than waiting until you have the courage to do big things for God, why not start by doing the small things right in front of you?

Bring up that conversation you've been avoiding. Donate to that charity you've been meaning to support. Start researching the small business you've been dreaming of for months now. Pick up the phone and call the single mom you've been meaning to reach out to. Email the local nonprofit you've wanted to volunteer with for some time now.

Don't wait until conditions are perfect, you have it all figured out, or you have all the time, money, and resources you'd like to donate to the cause. Don't wait until the morning you suddenly wake up brave and full of ambitions. Life doesn't work that way.

Instead, start small. Take the first step, then another, and then another, trusting that God will guide your path as you put your trust in Him and your faith into action.

What is one small step you can take to stand strong in your faith or to put that faith into action? Don't put it off any longer. Find your first step and start today!

9

Choosing Your Friendships Wisely

How should I navigate relationships
with non-Christians?

Fifteen years ago, before I was married, I trusted a close family friend to give me and my best friend a ride home from a popular summer festival downtown.

Instead of taking us home, however, he took us to a gay bar and wouldn't let us leave until we'd both had a few shots (enough to get us drunk). Then he drove us out to the middle of nowhere, scaring the living daylights out of me, before eventually delivering us home safe and sound.

Apparently, he thought this would be funny. I didn't think it was funny at all. I am no longer friends with this person, and I have no desire to be.

A few years later, another close family friend slowly slipped into alcoholism and drug use. Sadly, this meant my husband and I had to create distance from this person, though I miss him dearly and would love to be friends again.

In the last chapter, I encouraged you to surround yourself with committed Christians who encourage and inspire you to grow in your faith. However, this doesn't mean you can be friends *only* with people who hold the same values and make the same choices you do.

While most of our closest friends and family members are wonderful, committed Christians who love the Lord and seek to follow Him more closely every day, we do have several friends and family members who have chosen a different path.

We have multiple friends, family members, and acquaintances who battle drug and alcohol addictions, who have chosen LGBTQ lifestyles, who have walked out on their marriages, who have had abortions, who regularly lie to their spouses, who have committed credit card fraud, or who have been arrested for drug use, arson, robbery, or embezzlement.

No one's perfect. We all make mistakes, and our friends and family do too.

The question is, *How should we, as Christians, respond in these situations?*

Is it wise to maintain close relationships with people who consistently make choices we disagree with—whether in the areas of religion, politics, parenting, finances, or social justice?

How do we balance reaching out to a world in need (and not abandoning the friends and family we care about deeply) while still protecting ourselves and our children from being negatively influenced by the ideas, beliefs, values, and choices our post-Christian culture promotes and celebrates?

It almost feels silly to ask, "Should we, as Christians, be friends with people who believe differently than we do?" And yet, in today's ultrapolarized world, it's a question we're faced with every day.

Recently, I saw a news story in which a well-known celebrity proudly shared that she refuses to be friends with anyone who doesn't agree with her stance on a specific highly controversial issue. I've seen countless stories of parents and grandparents who refuse to attend their own children's or grandchildren's weddings, baptisms, or birthday parties due to differences in belief.

I even recently received an email from a lovely woman who wrote, "I wanted to love Equipping Godly Women. I can tell you put a lot of time and effort into it. However, I need to unsubscribe because you are friends with people who follow and share content from Christian leaders whose beliefs and actions I disagree with."

This reader wasn't even concerned about *my* beliefs. She opted out of our amazing community of Jesus-loving Christian women because she was concerned about how *my blogger friends* (who I've never even met in person) might be negatively influenced by the leaders *they* follow and how that might affect me.

Google the question "Can Christians be friends with non-Christians?" and you'll find a variety of conflicting articles written by authors who have very strong opinions on the matter.

Some articles nearly insist that befriending non-Christians is a surefire way to send yourself down a sinful path you can't possibly control, while others make a strong case that you can't witness to a world in need if you aren't willing to speak to the people living in it.

It isn't difficult to see where these conflicting views come from either.

The Bible has a great deal to say about the company we keep, and this advice can be confusing at first glance. Rather than dismiss it as contradictory, however, we want to dive in and examine the nuance.

Then, after we see what the Bible says on this topic, we'll look at five questions you can ask yourself to help determine the wisdom of pursuing a friendship with someone who believes differently than you do. Let's examine the verses together.

Dive Deeper into Scripture

→ Read 1 Corinthians 15:33; 2 Corinthians 6:14; and James 4:4. Why do these Bible verses caution against friendships with non-Christians? What is at risk?

→ Read Matthew 9:37–38; 10:16; 13:24–30. What relationship do these verses assume we will have with non-Christians? (Hint: Think beyond the obvious commands to the practical application.) Do these verses contradict the previous verses or add additional, clarifying information? How so?

Tamara's Story

Before I converted at forty-two, I lived with various boyfriends during grad school and then got married with babe in arms. I'm a Christian now, but my entire family is still secular and liberal.

My brother-in-law is gay and lives with a long-term partner, and I treat him exactly how I needed to be treated by Christians before my conversion—with love. No judgment, and no making statements by not spending time with him and his partner. I love him dearly.

My twenty-six-year-old niece lives with her boyfriend as well. She is asking questions about the faith. I am answering, recommending books, praying, and offering love, support, and guidance.

Because I was "loved and supported" into the faith—not "judged" into the faith—that's how I approach others.

Five Questions to Help You Navigate Relationships with Non-Christians

After studying multiple verses on this topic, we can reasonably conclude that God isn't calling us to completely separate ourselves from everyone who isn't living a perfect Christian life. Not only is that unrealistic, but it's also unloving.

Instead, we need to exercise biblical discernment and pray for the Holy Spirit's guidance in each of our interactions.

Here are five questions to ask yourself as you determine which relationships with friends and family would be wise to pursue, which you might gently let go, and how to navigate the tricky situations these relationships may put you in.

I. What Is the Person's Attitude toward Christianity?

Outside of Saturday morning cartoons, most people really can't be divided into "good guy" and "bad guy" categories. We're all complex human beings who make a variety of good and bad choices on a daily basis. We don't fall neatly into perfect groups.

That being said, much of the Bible's advice regarding our relationships with Christians and non-Christians relates to which of the following four groups the person generally tends to fall into:

- Christians who actively pursue God's will
- Non-Christians who aren't opposed to God's will
- Self-proclaimed Christians who actively reject God's will
- Non-Christians who actively reject God's will

Let's see what the Bible has to say about each of these key categories.

Christians Who Actively Pursue God's Will

This one comes as no surprise. The Bible contains multiple verses urging us to surround ourselves with strong, committed Christians who can give us wise, biblical advice and encouragement to help us grow in faith.

You certainly don't have to be friends with every Christian, but it is wise to surround yourself with a variety of Christian friends and mentors, if at all possible.

Dive Deeper into Scripture

→ Read Hebrews 10:24–25 and Acts 2:42–47. How is
your church similar or dissimilar to the early church as
described in these passages? How would the global
church be different if every Christian followed the
example set forth here?

Non-Christians Who Aren't Opposed to God's Will

Additionally, many non-Christians can make wonderful friends
as well—as long as they are respectful of your beliefs and share
similar values. The world is full of people who are kind, loving, and
compassionate but who don't consider themselves to be Christians
for whatever reason, and it would be a shame to miss out on their
friendship.

To give a personal example, one of my best friends in high school
was a Satanist who listened to heavy metal and wore all-black, full-
goth attire to school every day. We definitely did not share religious
beliefs.

Yet she always respected my strong Christian convictions and
never tried to influence me away from them. In fact, of all my
friends, she was the one who would bluntly call me out any time I
wasn't acting very Christlike. She held me accountable to what I said
I believed, often encouraged me to do the right thing, and definitely
kept me out of trouble more than once. While we lost touch over the
years, it was a very positive friendship for both of us.

Of course, it's important to note that I wasn't friends *only* with
Satanists. I was heavily involved in church, youth group, and Bible

study. I was part of a strong Christian family, and I had many Christian friends and role models.

Had I or my parents had any concerns about her influence in my life, that might have been different. But she wasn't the one my parents had to worry about—it was some of my "Christian" friends who were proving to be negative influences.

Dive Deeper into Scripture

→ Read Matthew 9:9–13 and Luke 7:37–39, 44–47. Why did Jesus choose to invest Himself in sinners? Why do you think this made the Pharisees so angry? What do you notice about the way Jesus treated those society considered "less than"?

Self-Proclaimed Christians Who Actively Reject God's Will

Perhaps the most difficult area to exercise discernment in is with friends and family who call themselves Christian but who live blatantly sinful lifestyles.

Some of the Bible's harshest and scariest words are reserved—not for non-Christians—but for self-proclaimed Christians who stubbornly and consistently act contrary to what the Bible teaches.

Of course, we know that no one is perfect. Scripture is full of stories of very godly men and women who temporarily acted in ungodly ways. And I've certainly had my fair share of times when I've gone directly against what I knew God was calling me to do as well. This is normal.

However, there's a big difference between trying (and failing) to follow God's perfect will and intentionally *choosing* to live in blatant sin while calling ourselves Christians. Persistent, unrepentant sin is not something God takes lightly.

While there are times when God may call us to maintain relationships with self-proclaimed Christians who aren't living a Christian lifestyle, this is one area where you will want to pray for discernment.

Dive Deeper into Scripture

→ Read I Corinthians 5:9–13 and 2 Thessalonians 3:6, 14–15. Who does Paul instruct us to judge? Who does Paul instruct us *not* to judge? Why does Paul give these commands? (Hint: What might happen if we don't follow his instructions?)

→ Read Revelation 3:14–19. Why would it be better to be "cold" in our faith, rather than "lukewarm"? What does God command these Christians to do (v. 19b)? Why?

Non-Christians Who Actively Reject God's Will

Last, if you have friends or family who are actively opposed to Christianity, talk terribly about the church or other Christians, or are regularly involved in unethical or illegal behavior, it may be wise to steer clear—unless you clearly feel the Holy Spirit prompting you to do otherwise.

Yes, there is a chance you could be the one to share the love of Christ with them (and if God prompts you to, please do!). But there are no biblical examples that show Christians befriending people who are *adamantly* opposed to Christianity over a period of time in hopes of winning them to Christ.

God never forces or compels anyone to love or follow Him who chooses not to, and we have no right or authority to insist others love or serve God either.

Dive Deeper into Scripture

→ Read Matthew 7:6. What is the main idea of this passage? When might you *not* want to share the gospel with an unbeliever? What might happen if you do "throw your pearls to pigs"?

→ Read Matthew 10:11–14. What type of person did Jesus instruct the disciples to seek out? How might they know if the person was worthy? What did Jesus command the disciples to do if the person was not? What application does this passage have for us today?

Claire's Story

When I was eighteen, I moved out of the apartment I shared with a friend because she was having an affair with a twenty-eight-year-old married man who had two small kids, and I didn't want to be a part of it.

She kept bringing him over to our place (to have sex in our shared bedroom), and in my young, inexperienced mind, my only choices were to bail or tell the wife. I didn't want the wife to "shoot the messenger," so I bailed, after telling my friend exactly why.

> My friend was super angry with me and didn't under-
> stand why I couldn't "just support her" as her friend. We
> stopped talking after that.

2. What Are My Own Personal Weaknesses, Limitations, and Areas of Temptation?

A few years ago, I wrote an article titled "Why Christians Belong in Bars."[1] The main idea was that if we want to reach a world in need, we need to go where they are.

Yes, this includes church outreach events, the grocery store, the bank, and the PTA, but it also includes prisons, bars, strip clubs, liquor stores, and the worst neighborhoods in town.

While most people agreed with the article, a few were appalled. "Good Christians don't belong in these places!" they insisted. "What if it caused them to sin? What if someone else saw them and it hurt their Christian witness?"

It's important to clarify: Yes, *some* Christians do need to go into prisons, bars, strip clubs, and liquor stores, but that does not mean *all* Christians are called to witness in these places. It's important to know your own personal limitations and prayerfully discern where God is calling you.

Personally, I've never found alcohol all that tempting. The idea of drinking to excess holds zero appeal to me (in large part due to the story I shared at the beginning of this chapter), and I have no problem showing moderation or restraint in this area. If I felt God calling me (or my husband) to befriend people at a bar, I would have no problem with that.

Yet there are other situations where it would not be wise for me to go.

I personally do not feel called to befriend gang members, sex traffickers, drug dealers, or violent prison inmates. As a young, relatively small female with no experience in any of these areas, this would not be wise for me. I also have to set certain boundaries and guidelines for myself as someone who has had an eating disorder in the past.

Valerie's Story

I've cut contact with friends and family when those relationships have led me toward sin. I'll hang out until I know I'm unable to handle it and then quietly bow out.

For example, my family is very political. I have to be honest with myself when I'm trying to take a splinter out of another's eye when I have a log in my own eye, so to speak. Or when I find myself in an echo chamber—surrounded only by people who think and believe like I do.

Do you have a personal or family history of drug or alcohol addiction? Do you have unhealed trauma that could make some sins more tempting for you? Are certain people, places, or situations triggering for you? Could pursuing ministry opportunities in these areas negatively impact your faith, your family, or your health? If so, then please steer clear.

But if God has called and uniquely gifted you with the life experience, skills, ability, or personality to help in these or other questionable situations—please do!

Dive Deeper into Scripture

→ Read James 1:13–15. According to this passage, how do we fall into sin? How might this process be slightly different for everyone?

→ Read 1 Corinthians 10:12–13. Why do we need to be careful when entering potentially tempting situations? How does God help us?

3. What Can I Reasonably Expect in This Situation?

If you do decide to form close friendships with people who aren't Christian, it would probably be wise to consider in advance how you will react to any potential beliefs or behavior you disagree with.

All too often, we expect our friends and family to act like Christians—even when they're not. If we believe the Holy Spirit empowers us to live godly lives, then it isn't fair to expect non-Christians to live godly lives without Him.

And if the reason we follow Christianity's rules and guidelines is because we love God and believe His way is best (this is why I follow them!), then it also isn't fair to expect others to follow Christianity's rules without a relationship with the One who inspires us to follow them in the first place.

It's fine to share what you believe. (We'll talk about this in the next chapter.) But it isn't fair to insist that others think, believe, or behave exactly as you do simply because you believe it's right or because it makes you more comfortable.

Are you okay being friends with someone even if it may put you in a tricky situation? Are you okay with having conversations with your children you may not otherwise need to have? Can you politely disagree on important issues without feeling offended, attacked, or persecuted? Are you okay setting boundaries where needed?

These are questions only you can answer.

Dive Deeper into Scripture

→ Read Ezekiel 36:26–27; John 14:16–17; and Galatians 5:22–23. What benefits does the Holy Spirit offer us as believers?

Vanessa's Story

My parents are manipulative, play a ton of games, and use their children to hurt their other children. They make many bad decisions, are very overwhelming, and don't respect anything I say.

I often have to take a deep breath and try not to over-react or get upset about the little things, but it's difficult when my family lies, steals, does drugs, and plays mind games. As a result, I've had to limit the time I spend with them.

Right now, I am taking it day by day. I haven't cut the strings completely because they are my children's grandparents. I do love them, so it's hard to watch, but at the same time, it can't be my problem. I can't save the world.

4. Do I Need to Set Firm Boundaries (and If So, Where)?

Once you've determined who you do (or do not) want to pursue a relationship with, the next step is to determine which type of relationship you'd like to have.

Rather than a simple yes or no answer, here are four more-nuanced options:

- **Close relationship:** You are good friends with this person. You can talk about anything, and you value their advice.
- **Casual relationship:** You want to spend time with this person, but you prefer to keep the conversation superficial. You avoid certain topics or situations.
- **Limited relationship:** You agree to spend time with this person—if and only if specific, predetermined boundaries are respected. For example, *if and only if* you meet in a public place, they don't bring up a certain topic, they haven't engaged in certain behaviors beforehand, or certain other people aren't around.

- **No relationship:** You choose not to have a relationship with this person in order to avoid the negative effects a relationship is likely to cause.

While setting and enforcing healthy boundaries can be difficult, it is completely biblical and sometimes necessary in order to salvage a damaged relationship or to protect yourself or your loved ones from the harm a potential relationship could cause.[2]

This is a decision you will need to make for yourself, under the guidance of the Holy Spirit and with the counsel and advice of other strong Christians who know the situation well.

Jen's Story

We've had to limit contact with my husband's brother, as he has untreated mental health issues and is an addict. It was too stressful (especially for my husband), as his family relied on him to take care of his brother's choices, even though his brother is independent and could hold a job if he wanted to.

We've also had to limit how much time we spend at his parents' home because everything always comes back to negative topics and his brother's issues.

It's difficult when I have to tell my daughter she has to go to day care instead of to her Nana's because my brother-in-law can become violent when on drugs. I know his parents have noticed, but we do try to spend some time there every couple of weeks.

5. How Are Your Friendships Affecting You?

And finally, no matter who you're friends with (Christian or not), it's important to regularly reevaluate the impact your friends are having on you—as well as the impact you're having on them.

Do your closest friends challenge, encourage, and inspire you to grow in your faith? Do they hold you accountable, point out your blind spots, and confront you when you're headed in the wrong direction? Are you more Christlike after spending time with them? Or do they regularly distract you from your faith or influence you to make negative choices you wouldn't otherwise make?

And alternately, what type of influence do you have on those around you? Do you truly help your friends grow in their relationship with Christ? Do you present a positive picture of Christianity that makes others curious to learn more? Or are you just another coworker to gossip and complain with?

Just because someone has been a part of your past does not mean they need to be a part of your future—especially if either of you is having a pronounced negative effect on the other.

Yes, you should be kind and loving to everyone. But that does not mean you must be best friends or spend a great deal of time with someone who is negatively impacting your mental, emotional, physical, or spiritual health.

Again, please seek the guidance of the Holy Spirit and the counsel of Christian friends and mentors who know you well when making these types of decisions.

Dive Deeper into Scripture

→ Read Galatians 2:11–14. Why did Paul rebuke Peter (Cephas)? Why was Peter behaving this way? What did Peter's choice say about his priorities?

→ Read Luke 19:1–9 and John 4:7–9, 27–30, 39–41. Who does Jesus spend time with in these passages? What effect do these encounters have on Jesus' faith, if any? What effect do they have on the people He spends time with?

IO

Witnessing with Truth and Love

*How can I share the gospel
without being weird or pushy?*

While Christianity is still the most common religion in America today, statistics show it's rapidly falling out of favor. According to Pew Research Center, only 65 percent of all American adults self-identify as Christian, compared to 77 percent just a decade before.[1]

This isn't due to a lack of knowledge.

According to David Kinnaman and Gabe Lyons, authors of *unChristian: What a New Generation Really Thinks about Christianity … and Why It Matters*, the vast majority of Americans have heard the gospel message at least once before. "Among non-Christians ages sixteen to twenty-nine … more than four out of every five have gone to a Christian church at some time in their life…. Most of these attended for at least three months."[2]

The issue isn't that people haven't heard or don't know what Christianity offers. For many, the problem is they've seen how

some self-proclaimed "Christians" think and behave, and they want nothing to do with it.

Christians have earned quite the reputation. Rather than being known for our love, generosity, or commitment to serving those in need, we're often seen as judgmental, closed-minded, hypocritical, ignorant, stubborn, or old-fashioned. We're seen as antihomosexual, antichoice, and antiscience. And according to many critics, we're too involved in politics and too focused on forcing our own thoughts and beliefs on others.[3]

This isn't to say all Christians are this way—far from it. But it isn't hard to see how Christians as a whole have gotten this negative reputation.

With easy, near-instant access to information from all around the globe right at our fingertips, one of our greatest challenges as Christians isn't to share facts and information the world doesn't know. Rather, it's presenting a more accurate picture of *"This is who God is. And this is what it can look like to follow Him today."*

This is both a tremendous opportunity and responsibility.

What Sharing the Gospel Is and Is Not

So how do we share the gospel with others—without being weird or pushy?

Before we unpack what effectively sharing the gospel *can* look like, we first need to look at what sharing the gospel is *not*.

It should go without saying, but sharing the gospel does not mean quoting Scripture at people, criticizing or shaming them for making decisions we disagree with, making snide remarks about others' choices under our breath or behind their backs, bluntly informing others they're going to hell if they don't change their beliefs or behavior, or insisting that others must think and behave exactly as we do (or suffer the consequences).

None of these are helpful, loving, or appropriate.

Sharing the gospel also does not mean forcing people to listen to our thoughts and beliefs when they don't care, pressuring them to make a one-time decision, or needing to answer every single question or objection someone may have even remotely related to Christianity.

Sharing the gospel is not a one-time event, and it's rarely a formal, structured conversation (though it can certainly lead to one).

The way you share your faith is going to vary depending on the person you're talking to—whether someone was once a strong believer but fell away, someone is adamantly opposed to the gospel, or someone is eager to learn more about the Christian faith for the first time.

But typically, talking about your faith is going to involve a fairly informal, natural conversation where you share a bit about your past experiences and current beliefs *when it's appropriate to do so.*

Michelle's Story

My dad had a cancer scare a while back.

Around that time, I started having some tooth issues. While I was sitting in the dentist's chair, I got a text that said the tests had come back and there was no cancer! I was so excited I gasped.

I apologized to the hygienist and shared the good news. She looked shocked and shared that her dad had been recently diagnosed with cancer. I listened for a few minutes and sympathized with her situation.

When I got ready to leave, I felt the Holy Spirit leading me to pray for her and her dad. I asked her if I could pray with her, and she happily agreed. She was crying by the end, and I have prayed that God would use that small thing in her life to lead her another step closer to Him.

How to Share the Gospel with Others

Here are six practical tips to help you share what you believe with others—in a way that is helpful, genuine, and likely to be well received, not pushy, rude, or annoying.

I. Remember Your Role in the Salvation Process

First, you'll want to approach the conversation with the right mindset and perspective.

It's important to remember: It is not your responsibility to "save" anyone or to convince anyone to think, believe, or act the way you do. Jesus is our *only* Savior, and it's His job to soften hearts, not ours. Our role, as Christians, is simply to share what we know and have experienced (to the extent that the other person is open to hearing it), not to convince or force others to listen or agree.

Remember, the person you are speaking with is a human being made in God's image with inherent worth, dignity, and free will. As desperately as you may want them to also follow Jesus, it's ultimately their choice to make—not yours.

So please feel free to share your hard-earned wisdom, beliefs, and advice with those who seem interested in learning more, while also respecting the wishes of those who do not.

Donna's Story

I have shared the gospel with people who I know are not believers. I am careful about how I do it, however, because some people will block out anything you have to say if you are too "confrontational" toward them.

I often tell people that it is because of the grace of God that I am able to stay positive in spite of the circumstances I am facing right now. If they seem receptive to hearing me share, I take the opportunity to do so.

Dive Deeper into Scripture

→ Read I Corinthians 3:4–9. What does the seed represent in this passage? How do these two men work together with God?

→ Read Ezekiel 11:17–21. What does God promise to do
in this passage? How might this promise apply to us
today? (Think: main idea.)

2. Pray for Wisdom and Guidance

Next, you want to make sure to cover your conversations in prayer.

While you may never fully know or understand the specific reasons your friends, family, or acquaintances may choose not to accept
a relationship with the God who loves them, God does.

Therefore, it only makes sense to ask God for His wisdom and
guidance as you navigate these potentially tricky conversations.

For example, you can pray:

- for wisdom to say the right thing
- that God would speak to both of you loudly and
  clearly
- that you would be willing to listen to Him and
  each other
- that you would be humble enough to admit when
  you're wrong
- that God would make His presence and provision
  undeniable
- that God would give you the strength and courage to make wise decisions even when it's hard

Whether or not your friends, family members, or acquaintances
choose to live as believers is ultimately between them and God. But

we can always ask God for wisdom, direction, and the softening of our hearts and those of others.

Dive Deeper into Scripture

→ Read I Kings 3:5–14 and James 1:5. What does Solomon ask for in I Kings 3? How does God respond? What do these passages tell us about God's character?

3. Share Your Story and Experiences

As I mentioned earlier, sharing your faith is rarely (if ever) about sitting someone down to deliver a formal, structured presentation on the benefits of following Jesus Christ as your Lord and Savior.

Rather, it typically involves sharing your own story, experience, and knowledge when it's appropriate to do so. I can assure you it doesn't have to be weird, scary, or unnatural, and it does get easier with time and practice.

If you can comfortably share restaurant recommendations, talk about what you did over the weekend, or give a coworker advice, you can share your faith in a similar way.

For example, you could invite a friend to join you for church, a Christian concert, a Bible study, or an outreach event you're excited to attend. You could mention a Christian book you've read recently, why you loved it, and what you learned from it.

Or you could share a story about how God has come through in your life in the past. For example, you might say something like, "When I was in my twenties, I went through a rough period when

I was into drugs, sex, and alcohol. My life was a mess. Thankfully, a friend invited me to church, I gave my life to Christ, and it has made an incredible difference! I love knowing I'm not alone."

Similarly, you could share your biblical wisdom, perspective, or advice with a friend, family member, or coworker going through a challenging situation, if they seem open to it. You could share Scripture verses you find encouraging or let others see how you cling to God's promises in the struggles you're currently facing.

You could let friends, family, coworkers, or acquaintances know you're praying for them and ask if there is anything specific they'd like you to pray for. Or you might simply find ways to quietly love and serve those in your community through donating your time, talent, or resources to those in need.

Sharing your faith doesn't have to mean presenting others with the entire gospel message—although there is a time and place for that. Instead, it often means showing people in the context of a relationship: this is what following Christ can look like today.

Dive Deeper into Scripture

→ Read John 9:13–17, 24–25. How did the formerly blind man share his faith with the Pharisees? (Did he provide a lengthy argument, a long list of Bible verses, or answers to all their questions?) What does this man's example tell us about the way we might share our faith today?

→ Read Matthew 5:13–16. What does it mean to be "the light of the world"? How might your actions provide light to the world around you?

4. Know the Gospel

Once you begin having more conversations about your faith, you may find that people *do* want to know more. These opportunities can pop up seemingly out of nowhere, so it makes sense to prepare in advance.

If someone asks what you believe and why, do you know how to share the gospel accurately and succinctly, without missing any major points?

One of the most common pitfalls many people run into is presenting the gospel as a life-improvement plan: *"Just trust Jesus as your personal Lord and Savior, and He'll make all your problems go away!"* This messaging is problematic for a number of reasons.

First, it assumes that the only people who need Christianity are those who are currently facing a significant challenge or problem. Second, it runs completely against Jesus' warning that "in this world you will have trouble."[4] And third, it misses most of the true gospel message.

Here is one way I might explain the key points of the gospel message to an interested nonbeliever. (Feel free to adapt to your audience as needed!)

1. There is one God in three persons (God the Father, Jesus the Son, and the Holy Spirit), who created the heavens, the earth, and everything in them (Gen. 1).

2. As the Creator of the universe, God knows how it works best. We don't always know why He makes the decisions He does, but we can trust that God

is good and His laws are always in our best interests (Isa. 55:8–9; Ex. 34:6).

3. While God is perfect, we are not. And as imperfect human beings, we've all gone against God's
will for our lives at some point. The Bible calls
this "sin" (Rom. 3:23).

4. The Bible tells us sin has serious consequences,
both eternally and here on earth. Because God is
holy, our sin separates us from Him (Rom. 6:23;
Isa. 59:2).

5. Thankfully, God loves us so much that He sent His
Son, Jesus, to take the eternal punishment (or consequences) for our sin on our behalf (Rom. 5:8).

6. God doesn't force us to love Him or worship
Him. He freely offers us forgiveness for our sins
and a right relationship with Him through His
Son, Jesus, but it's up to us to accept it (John
3:16; Eph. 2:8–9).

7. While we can never earn our salvation (it's a free
gift given by grace through faith), if we believe
God is who He says He is and His way is best, we
will naturally *want* to do good works because we
love Him (Matt. 16:24; James 2:14–26).

Dive Deeper into Scripture

→ Read Acts 2:1–4, 14–17, 40–41. How does Peter share
the gospel in this passage? How is his approach

different than the Samaritan woman's approach we see in John 4:27–42? Why do you think these two people used two different approaches?

→ After reading the verses listed above, how might you share the gospel message with a non-Christian who wanted to learn more?

Betty's Story

Years ago, a coworker and dear friend of mine attempted suicide after she was diagnosed with multiple sclerosis. I went and visited her at her home, and we began reading the Bible together.

After about three months of studying God's Word together, she gave her heart to the Lord. Her son brought her to church, and she was baptized. I hugged her and told her that she was part of the family of God and that we would be here for her. A few months later, she passed away.

I'm so thankful I made the effort to go see her and talk with her about her salvation, and I know I'll see her again in glory one day.

5. Know the Answers to Common Questions

In addition to knowing how to present the gospel succinctly, it's also wise to know the answers to some of the most common questions or objections people have regarding Christianity today.

For example, what would you say if someone responded with "Christians are hypocrites," "Why do Christians hate gay people?" or "How can you believe in a religion that treats women like objects?"

Consider the difference between these two replies: "That's ridiculous! How could you say that?" versus "Yeah. There definitely are some hypocritical people in the church. It bothers me too, and God doesn't like it either. But that's one thing I do love about the church. No matter how broken or messed up we are—and we all are in some way—God loves each of us anyway. We're all works in progress, and we all need Jesus. That's why we go to church."

Tracy's Story

I have close friends who do things I don't agree with. I simply remind myself that I once participated in similar sins too and I somehow found my way. And even though I am no longer participating in the same sins my friends are participating in (such as sex outside of marriage), I still have sins that I struggle with.

I am thankful for those who prayed for me and loved me even when I struggled to love myself. Now I continue to love my friends and pray for them, while being careful to avoid enabling their behavior in the process.

The first reply above denies any validity to the person's fears or concerns. It refuses to take responsibility and instead sweeps important concerns under the rug.

The second answer acknowledges the very real problem, making the person feel heard while shifting the perspective back to where it belongs: *"Yes, people mess up. We're human. Thankfully, we serve a God who is above all that."*

Alternately, if someone asks you a question you don't know how to answer, it's completely fine to say, "That's a great question! Let me look into it and get back to you."

No one expects you to know everything, and honestly, it hurts your witness if you pretend you do. We're all growing and learning, and that's okay.

Yet it can be very helpful to research in advance some of the most common objections or questions you're likely to get.[5]

Dive Deeper into Scripture

→ Read I Peter 3:15–16. In what ways do non-Christians commonly slander Christians today? How would you answer these accusations?

6. Be Sensitive to Controversial Issues

Have you ever heard the saying "People don't care how much you know until they know how much you care"?

This phrase could not be truer than when discussing how non-Christians view the church's stances on controversial topics including abortion, LGBTQ rights, divorce, gender roles, immigration laws, racial justice, and many other issues debated by society.

People already know the church's traditional position on issues like these. Simply telling someone, "Abortion is murder," "Adam and Eve, not Adam and Steve," or responding, "Well, the Bible says …"

really isn't helpful, especially if you're speaking to a non-Christian who isn't particularly interested in what the Bible has to say.

Remember: **We don't follow God's laws so that we can have a relationship with Him. We follow God's laws because we have a relationship with Him.**

Yes, there are certainly times when it is appropriate to confront people in sin. (We'll talk about this in the next chapter.) But this rarely happens publicly on social media or in angry arguments.

Instead, we need to check our motivation. Are we acting out of genuine love and concern for people who don't know the life-changing power of Jesus? Or are we more concerned with making sure everyone else agrees with and upholds the same beliefs and values we do?

Jesus never demanded nonbelievers follow God's laws. Instead, He treated them with dignity and respect, showed them He cared, and *then* told them to "go and sin no more."

We would be wise to do the same.

Dive Deeper into Scripture

→ Read John 8:3–11. How did the crowd treat the woman caught in adultery? How did Jesus? Did Jesus break the law in this passage? What does this passage tell us about His view of the law?

→ Read Matthew 23:1–7, 23, 27–28. Why do you think Jesus responded so differently to the woman caught in adultery and the Pharisees, when both were guilty of sin? When might it be appropriate to use one response over the other?

You Have a Responsibility to Share the Gospel

While sharing the gospel can certainly be nerve-racking (especially at first!), I don't believe Jesus intended it to be optional. As we saw in chapter 2, one of the four main commands Jesus gave His disciples was to go make more disciples, and this command still applies to us today.

Plus, if we truly believe the gospel message ourselves, it only makes sense that we would want to share it with others.

Think about it this way: If you saw a toddler fall into a pool, would you just sit there while he drowned? If a fire broke out in a building you were in, would you try to sneak out quietly? If you discovered the cure for cancer, would you keep it to yourself?

Every day, people all around us are dying—whether physically, spiritually, or emotionally. If we truly believe that faith is necessary not only for eternal life but also for a purposeful and meaningful life here on earth, wouldn't we want to share that?

This doesn't mean we need to lead *every* person we meet to Christ, of course. We shouldn't view others as "projects," and as we've already discussed, God saves—not us.

But if we *truly* believe the gospel message and we *truly* love other people, then we should want to share this good news with others as often as we can. If we don't feel compelled to share the good news with those around us, we may want to ask ourselves, *Why not?*

Dive Deeper into Scripture

→ Read Romans 1:13–15; 10:12–15. Why did Paul consider himself "obligated both to Greeks and non-Greeks"

(1:14)? Why do you think he shared the gospel so boldly, despite the very real religious persecution he faced throughout his ministry?

→ Read Matthew 28:16–20. Were all of Jesus' disciples confident and full of faith? What reassurance did Jesus give them? How might this passage apply to our lives today?

11

Speaking Up against Sin and Wrongdoing

When should I confront others' sin, and how?

"What do you think, Brittany? What would you do if it were your kid?"

It wasn't unusual for the women in our moms' group to take turns sharing openly and honestly about the very real issues they faced each week, in hopes of receiving wise advice and encouragement from friends who cared. But this question had us all stumped.

Despite being raised in a Christian home, one woman's son had recently come out as transgender, and she wasn't sure how to respond. Unfortunately, none of us knew either.

Should she respect his decision, using his new preferred pronouns and allowing him to dress however he pleased? Should she insist he behave more in line with his Christian upbringing, refusing to allow him to wear dresses and makeup to church or to school?

What if it was just a phase? What if it wasn't? What if this tore their relationship apart? What if her son turned his back on God, never to return? What would this decision mean for her son's future or for their family as a whole?

It was obvious the woman cared deeply about her child. All the other moms did too. But none of us knew how to help her make this incredibly tough decision, one with serious consequences that could affect her child for the rest of his life.

Have you ever been in a situation like this?

Maybe you have a friend or family member who has walked away from their faith to pursue an alternate lifestyle. Maybe you recently discovered your teen's secret stash of cigarettes, alcohol, porn, or drugs. Maybe you learned your best friend's husband is having an affair, your coworker is considering abortion, your neighbor is committing tax fraud, or your teenage niece is dating (and probably sleeping with) someone twice her age.

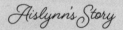

Aislynn's Story

Before returning to Jesus, I was a believer of "live and let live." I thought that by accepting others' lifestyles, I was showing love like Jesus did—through nonjudgment and compassion. I never tried to witness to my friends or let them know they are going against what God made as an honorable union.

I still struggle to discern between loving them and hating their sin, and I have not yet confronted anyone over their lifestyle, but I do pray they come to Jesus, repent, and turn from their sinful ways.

Alternately, maybe you have a friend or family member who isn't guilty of sin, necessarily, but who's currently facing a tricky situation that has the potential to significantly impact her life or the lives of those around her.

How should you respond to a friend who won't leave a toxic relationship or a family member who refuses to accept the help or medication he needs to treat his addiction, mental health issues, or past trauma?

And what about the blatant sin you see around you every day—on social media, in the news, in your workplace, or even in your church? Should you say something? And if so, what?

Should Christians Judge Others?

Whether out of genuine love and concern for others or a fear of being seen as judgmental, hypocritical, or rude, the "live and let live" attitude Aislynn describes in her story above is a common stance held by many in our society.

In fact, even non-Christians will commonly reference Bible verses like Matthew 7:1, which states, "Do not judge, or you too will be judged."

Alternately, you might hear "Who am I to judge?"—a question that comes from either 1 Corinthians 5:12, which begins, "What business is it of mine to judge," or James 4:12, which ends, "Who are you to judge your neighbor?"

In light of verses like these and others, many people strongly believe that Christians should never judge anyone—themselves or others. However, we must always be careful not to take individual verses out of context, distorting their meaning in the process.

The Bible has a great deal more to share on this topic than just these three verses, and it's a conversation filled with a great deal of nuance.

Let's dive deeper into Scripture together to see what the Bible says about judging others.

Dive Deeper into Scripture

→ Read I Corinthians 5:9–13. How does reading this passage in context affect the meaning of the phrase "Who am I to judge"? Whom does Paul say we should and should not judge in this passage?

→ Read Matthew 7:1–5. How does reading this passage in context affect your understanding of verse 1? Is Jesus instructing us *never* to judge? What does He instruct us to do?

→ Read Leviticus 19:15; Deuteronomy 16:18; Proverbs 31:8–9; and Galatians 6:1. What do these verses say about judging others? What would happen in our society if we could *never* judge any behaviors as right or wrong?

When Should We Confront Others in Sin?

In light of the verses in the section above, we can reasonably conclude that there are times when we, as Christians, have both a right and a responsibility to confront the sin and destructive choices we see in others' lives.

However, this does *not* mean we should make a habit of constantly criticizing every fault we find in those around us, nor does this mean we can speak our minds freely without consequence. We must exercise discernment, in both what we say and how we say it.

After all, there's a big difference between judging a specific *behavior* as right or wrong (which the Bible *does* instruct us to do) and treating a *person* judgmentally or with contempt (which the Bible does *not* instruct us to do).

This is why Colossians 4:6a tells us, "Let your conversation be always full of grace."

And Ephesians 4:29 instructs, "Do not let any unwholesome talk come out of your mouths, but only what is helpful for building others up according to their needs, that it may benefit those who listen."

Our goal in speaking up about sin should *never* be to embarrass, belittle, or insult the other person but rather to build up and encourage each other toward holy living, to the benefit of all.

With that in mind, here are six questions you can ask yourself to determine if, when, and how you might decide to speak up against the sin and wrongdoing you see in the world.

I. Why Do I Want to Speak Up?

Before you say anything, it's helpful to examine your motives and choose your words carefully.

For example, are you genuinely concerned for a friend or family member's well-being? Do you sincerely want what's best for them? Are you hoping to encourage them in their faith, their health, or their relationships?

Or is the real reason you're speaking up that you're angry, annoyed, or offended and you think that speaking your mind will make *you* feel better?

Is your desire to address others' sin secretly rooted in selfishness, self-centeredness, or pride? Are you more concerned with making sure others adhere to *your* Christian values, beliefs, opinions, rules, or preferences—even if they disagree—rather than focusing on loving others well? (Remember those Pharisees from chapter 1?)

If you're genuinely concerned for your friend or family member's well-being, then saying something may be the right option. However, if your desire to speak up comes primarily from selfish motives, you may need to ask God to work on your heart before you worry about someone else's.

Dive Deeper into Scripture

→ Read Mark 2:13–17; 3:1–6. What are the Pharisees most concerned about in these passages? What is Jesus most concerned about? What does this tell you about what God values?

2. Is the Behavior Clearly a Sin?

When I was growing up in a small, legalist church environment, it felt like nearly everything was a sin.

According to my youth leaders, I wasn't allowed to dance, wear tank tops, or be alone with a member of the opposite sex at any time for any reason. And I *certainly* wasn't allowed to drink, smoke, gamble, or spend time with people who did (unless I was inviting them to church, where they could repent of their "heathen ways").

At the time, I accepted these rules without question.

But as I grew up, I started to notice that not everyone (even truly devout, God-loving Christians) felt compelled to follow the long list of strict rules I'd always been taught were nonnegotiable for any good Christian who wanted to please the Lord.

In fact, Christians frequently disagree over which behaviors are and are not sinful, and it's entirely possible that a behavior you've deemed off-limits may be considered perfectly appropriate by someone else.

Clearly, we should take God's Word seriously and do our best to live according to it. God's commands are not optional.

But this requirement does not extend to the long list of additional, extrabiblical rules that many of us well-meaning Christians have created for ourselves and others. (Remember the Mishnah from chapter 1?)

For this reason, if the Bible doesn't clearly state that a certain behavior you want to address is immoral, it may be more effective to start a discussion rather than outright accusing others of sin. Perhaps the other person doesn't believe the behavior is a sin at all. And perhaps they're right.

For example, it is not inherently sinful to support one political candidate over another, to attend one type of church over another, or to support a controversial cause others disagree with. It is not sinful to feel anger, disappointment, disgust, sexual arousal, or the temptation to sin.

Life is messy, and religion is nuanced. And yet, how often do we accuse others of moral failure simply because they've researched the facts and come to a different conclusion than us?

This is why it's so important to approach others with love and grace in a genuine attempt to better understand their position, rather than immediately jumping to conclusions.

Dive Deeper into Scripture

→ Read I Corinthians 8:4–13; 10:23–33. How can certain actions be sinful for some but not others? How did Paul decide which behaviors are and are not okay (vv. 31–33)?

3. Am I Guilty of the Same Sin (or Others)?

I love the wisdom we see in Matthew 7:5b. It says, "Take the plank out of your own eye, and then you will see clearly to remove the speck from your brother's eye."

This passage doesn't mean we can't confront others if we have sin in our own lives. We can and should. But we need to start by acknowledging our own sin first.

When we start by addressing our own sin, it forces us to be humble and compassionate, rather than judgmental, arrogant, or condescending. It reminds us that we're all human and we all want love, patience, and grace as we grow.

It gives us a chance to see if we may be biased, along with the opportunity to determine any role we may have played in the situation. It also allows us time to rationally assess the situation, rather than responding quickly out of annoyance, anger, or fear.

Truthfully, there have been *many* times in my own life when I've initially been angry or annoyed with someone for a behavior, only to realize I'm guilty of the same behavior (or something comparable).

When this happens, I have two options. I can choose to overlook the other person's offense and focus my efforts on improving myself. (As I tell my children when they tattle or boss each other around, "Worry about yourself.") Or I can bring the issue to the other person as something we both need to work on, possibly together.

Either way, by taking time to examine my own conscience first, I can avoid an awkward situation where I'm unintentionally acting like a self-righteous hypocrite.

Dive Deeper into Scripture

→ Read Matthew 7:1–2 and Romans 2:1–5. What risk do we bring upon ourselves when we judge others?

→ Read James 5:19–20. What do we risk when we refuse to speak up?

Kathy's Story

I have friends and family who have deliberately chosen a life of sin and turned away from God. Before I say anything to them, the first and most important thing I do is to rightly align my heart with God, making sure that I have the proper perspective.

I must remember that I once was like they were, except for the grace of God granting me eyes to see and a repentant and regenerate heart. I must approach people with a humble and contrite heart, knowing that all have fallen short of the glory of God, including me.

> Once my heart is right, only then can I approach them and seek to restore them. I tell them how much I care, what I am feeling for them, what I fear and what I see, and that I am compelled by the Lord to say something, for if anything happened to them, I could not live with myself, and He would be so disheartened with me.
>
> I would then share my concerns, hug them, and end the conversation with them having a certainty that they are loved and cared for.

4. Is This Person a Christian?

One major benefit of having an elementary education degree is the fact that I can almost always help my children not only complete their homework but also understand what they're learning.

Whether they're counting by fives, identifying participle phrases, solving complex algebra equations, or conjugating Spanish verbs ... any time they can't complete an assignment on their own, I know how to help. Having a former teacher for a mom comes in very handy for my kids (and it's fun for me to see what I still remember).

As Christians, we have a Helper readily available as well.

John 14:26 tells us, "But the Advocate, the Holy Spirit, whom the Father will send in my name, will teach you all things and will remind you of everything I have said to you."

Furthermore, Romans 8:26 tells us, "In the same way, the Spirit helps us in our weakness. We do not know what we ought to pray for, but the Spirit himself intercedes for us through wordless groans."

This is so encouraging! But it also brings up an important point. If we truly believe that the Holy Spirit helps us (as Christians) in our weakness, then it's completely unfair to expect non-Christians to be able to live up to the same standard that we ourselves are unable to achieve, even though we have the Spirit's help.

Furthermore, **as Christians, we follow God's laws *because* we believe in Him, not *so that* we can believe in Him.** Why would we expect people to obey laws from a book they don't believe in or listen to a God they don't necessarily believe exists?

Yes, God's truth is unchanging, whether people believe in it or not. And there is definitely a time and place to confront others with the reality of their sin and the good news of the gospel.

However, we cannot expect non-Christians to blindly obey countercultural commands they've never seen a good reason to follow or shame them when they don't.

The desire to obey God flows out of our relationship with Him, not the other way around.

Dive Deeper into Scripture

→ Read Romans 8:1–8. What was the law powerless to do? What do verses 7–8 say about non-Christians' ability to please God apart from His Spirit (i.e., through their works)? What implications does this have for the way we confront non-Christians in sin?

→ Read Galatians 5:22–23. What is the natural result of a life lived according to the Spirit? Does this passage imply non-Christians can never do or be these things? If not, what is this passage saying?

5. How Much Authority or Influence Do I Have with This Person?

Once you've determined that an issue is worth addressing, the next question is, *Are* you *the best person to address it? How much authority or influence do you have in this person's life?*

If you're a parent with children living at home, you have tremendous influence and authority in their lives. You have both the right and the responsibility to raise them well.

Similarly, if you are a pastor, teacher, boss, or elected leader, you have both the right and the responsibility to lead those under your care.

Furthermore, you likely also have a high degree of influence with your spouse, parents, siblings, in-laws, and any other close friends, family members, or coworkers who value your opinion and insight.

However, while God has placed you in a position of influence over some people, He has not called you to a position of influence or authority over all.

If you don't have a real connection to the person you're considering speaking to—for example, if the person is a casual acquaintance, celebrity, politician, author, influencer, or a random stranger online—you may not be the person God has called to confront this person about this particular sin. Instead, it may be wise to pray for discernment and examine your motives (going back to step 1 in this list).

If you clearly hear the Holy Spirit prompting you to speak up, please do (politely). Otherwise, you don't have to involve yourself in every instance of sin or wrongdoing you see. Sometimes it's best to simply focus on those you have a personal connection with.

Dive Deeper into Scripture

→ Read Proverbs 22:6; Romans 13:1-2; James 3:1; and
1 Peter 3:1; 5:1-5. Who has God put you personally in
a position of authority over or influence with? Who
has God placed in authority over you?

6. Do I Know the Whole Story?

Recently, I had to have a difficult conversation with a friend who was repeatedly making harmful choices, negatively affecting both her life and the lives of those around her.

I put off the conversation for as long as I could, hoping she would recognize the consequences of her actions and the situation would resolve on its own. But when it didn't, I knew I had to speak up.

While the initial conversation was a bit rocky, it was also incredibly eye-opening. I realized that the harmful behavior I saw wasn't the real issue. It was merely a symptom of something deeper that was going on in her life at the time.

This didn't excuse her behavior and suddenly make it okay. It was still harmful, and she still needed to stop. But once I knew the underlying reason behind her behavior, it completely changed the conversation we needed to have.

Is it possible that those around you have reasons for their attitudes, choices, or behaviors that you know nothing about?

Maybe they're reacting to past trauma or current extenuating circumstances or pressures you aren't aware of. Maybe they've already made a ton of progress in this area but haven't fully arrived at their goal yet. Maybe they have additional information or a different perspective you haven't considered.

It's easy to write others off as wrong, uneducated, stubborn, or selfish when they support a political candidate, law, health care mandate, religious belief, or decision you strongly disagree with, but do you know how they came to their conclusion or what pressures they faced along the way? You may not.

While sin is sin regardless of the circumstances, knowing a bit more of the person's background or thought process, rather than assuming, can dramatically change the conversation. You don't want to assume.

Dive Deeper into Scripture

→ Read James 1:19 and Proverbs 18:13, 17. What do these passages imply we should do before we confront another's behavior? Why is this so important?

How to Address Others' Sin

One of the reasons I hesitated so long (several months, in fact) to have the difficult conversation I mentioned above is that I didn't know the best way to share what I wanted to say.

I didn't want to come across as judgmental, accusatory, or uncaring. I didn't want my friend to hear the wrong message, overreact, and make a bunch of other changes I wasn't requesting. I didn't want to jeopardize our relationship or ruin future plans we had together. And I didn't want her to feel like she couldn't be open and honest with me in the future, out of a fear that I was silently judging her or her choices.

I simply wanted her to see how her actions were affecting those around her, and I wanted to encourage her to live up to the amazing person she is and the person I know she wants to be. As difficult as this conversation would be, I knew I'd want my closest friends and family to do the same for me.

Are you feeling prompted to address a sin or wrongdoing you see around you? If so, there are six options available to you.

Let's go over each of these options in detail, starting with the most direct approach, so you can determine which one may be best for your situation.

I. You Can Speak to the Person Directly

After answering each of the six questions above—if you've examined your own motives, heart, and expectations, you've determined that the behavior is clearly a sin, you have some degree of influence or authority in their life, and you are confident you know the whole story—then it's likely appropriate (or even necessary) for you to speak up in love.

In fact, the Bible lays out a step-by-step process for addressing fellow believers in sin in Matthew 18:15–17: First, speak to the person privately. If that doesn't work, ask a few friends or family members to approach the person with you. If the person caught in sin still isn't receptive, you may need to get the authorities involved (for example, a pastor, priest, boss, or even the police for criminal matters).

This method can certainly be the most confrontational and therefore the most difficult, but it doesn't have to be. Depending on the nature and severity of the issue in question, as well as your relationship with the person, you may insist on changes, or you may simply lovingly express your concerns and leave the final decision for change up to them.

Dive Deeper into Scripture

→ Read Matthew 18:15–17. What process does the Bible give us for dealing with other Christians engaged in sinful behavior? How might following this process be necessary or beneficial?

→ Read Acts 5:1–11. What gave Peter the right to confront Ananias and Sapphira about their sin? Why did their sin need to be addressed? (Consider where this story is in the Bible—early Acts.)

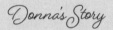

Donna's Story

I have a coworker who says she is a Christian, who shares about her faith, but who also openly shares how she is sexually involved with a married man.

There have been many times that I have "called her out" because of the things she tells me. I have told her that adultery is a sin, that she needs to work on her relationship with God, that she needs to talk to Him about what she is doing, and that she needs to make things right. I stop her when she wants to give me the details.

I've distanced myself from her because of these things (and a few others), but I haven't cut her off completely. I continue to pray for her and limit our conversations to work-related or faith-related topics. I do send her Bible verses and inspirational quotes to remind her of what God wants her to do.

It's not always easy to stand up to her and tell her these things. I told her it isn't my job to judge her and I'm not perfect either.

But as her friend, I need to be honest with her about her choices.

2. You Can Ask Questions

Going back to the six questions above, if you've determined that the behavior isn't necessarily sinful, you aren't close to the person, or you don't know the person's story, you may choose to simply ask questions rather than confront.

As I shared in *Fall in Love with God's Word*, this was the technique my Catholic mother-in-law used with me to start a discussion about our faith differences, and it worked really well.

Rather than telling me, "You're wrong!" she simply asked questions. She was polite, humble, and respectful, and I could tell she genuinely wanted to learn more about what I believed and why.

As a result, I never felt defensive, cornered, attacked, or manipulated. Instead, we both learned a lot, and I went on to do additional research on my own. Now I was curious too!

By taking the time to ask a few clarifying questions, you allow the other person to come to their own conclusions, and if there's even a chance you've misjudged the situation, you can quickly clarify any misunderstandings.

The other person may choose not to answer your questions, and they may never change their mind, but asking questions can be a good, nonconfrontational way to keep the communication open and let someone know you care.

3. You Can Share Your Own Personal Experience

Alternately, you may choose to open up about your own story, particularly if you have experience in the area the other person appears to be struggling with.

This way, you aren't asking or telling the other person to do or believe anything. You're simply sharing what you've been through and the lessons you learned along the way. What the other person does with this information is completely up to them.

For example, you might mention that you previously struggled with a drug addiction, your first marriage was abusive, or you had a hard time trusting God after your son died at an early age. You might share how you used to party, how you struggled financially, or how you learned to manage a debilitating mental illness.

If the other person seems interested, you could gently guide the conversation to include your faith and how it helped you both then and today—but no pressure. You simply want to let the other person know that you care, you understand what they're going through, and you'd be happy to share your experience and advice if they want to know more.

4. You Can Take the Issue to God in Prayer

While there are certainly times when a direct conversation is necessary, there are also times when it may not be a realistic or effective option.

For example, what if your teenage daughter has fallen in with the wrong crowd and she's refusing to listen to anything you say? What if your best friend's husband recently left her family for a younger woman he met online? What if you're concerned about the policy a political candidate may sign into law once she's elected into office?

In situations like these, your best course of action may simply be to take the issue to God in prayer. In fact, the Bible encourages us to do so in verses such as 1 Timothy 2:1–4. This passage reads:

> I urge, then, first of all, that petitions, prayers, intercession and thanksgiving be made for all people—for kings and all those in authority, that we may live peaceful and quiet lives in all godliness and holiness. This is good, and pleases God our Savior, who wants all people to be saved and to come to a knowledge of the truth.

Yes, there is a chance God may not answer our prayers the way we want Him to. God has given us all free will, and He won't force anyone to love Him who doesn't want to. But this doesn't mean we shouldn't try. He wants us to bring our requests to Him.

After all, if anyone can soften someone's heart, it's God.

Dive Deeper into Scripture

→ Read John 17:1, 15-17, 20-21. What did Jesus pray for Himself (v. 1), His disciples (vv. 15-17), and all

the believers (vv. 20–21)? Do you believe God has
answered His prayer? Why or why not?

→ Read Ezekiel 36:22–27. What did the Lord promise
to do for the Israelites? Why did He make them this
promise, even though they didn't deserve it?

Crystal's Story

Ever since I was a young girl, I've always been attracted to
other girls. I suppressed it for years (as I was raised in a
Christian home with a minister for a father), but once I
became an adult and left home, I finally gave in. I spent
years living an inappropriate lifestyle and hiding it from
those closest to me.

Because of my same-sex attraction, I felt I was an
abomination who couldn't be accepted by Christ.

As a result, I left the church, quit reading the Bible, and
even started questioning God's existence. I became involved
in explicit relationships and nearly ruined my marriage to
my wonderful husband.

It was only a little over a year ago that I did a complete
turnaround. I can't even explain how it happened.

I wasn't looking, I wasn't reading, and wasn't asking
anyone for advice. I just felt a push deep inside that made
me start to question what I was doing. I started having a
hunger for the relationship I used to have with Christ as a

child, and I was tired of the emptiness, the judgments, and the distance between me and my God.

I cried out to God, and He answered me. He told me that I was wrong, but He didn't yell at me or call me an abomination.

Instead, He told me He loved me. And He told me that in order for me to have that relationship with Him again and to receive the blessings He has for me, I had to give that up. I was more than willing to leave it at His feet.

I'm still learning how to be this new creation in Christ, and it isn't easy to walk, but I know He's there with me every step of the way.

5. You Can Choose to Ignore the Behavior

As a perfectionist, I always have a *long* list of ways I want to improve. Unfortunately, no matter how hard I try, I've come to accept that I will never be perfect. I'm only human, and there's only so much I can do.

And the same is true of everyone we see around us every day. We all have room for improvement, and we always will. Nobody's perfect.

This is why, in some cases, you may choose to simply overlook or ignore certain sins without saying anything at all—whether to God or the other person. This option is especially relevant if the sin is minor, the person isn't a Christian, you have no influence or authority in the person's life, or you don't know the situation.

Just because you see someone sin does not mean *you* always need to be the one to point it out. Sometimes you simply need to release it to God.

Dive Deeper into Scripture

→ Read Romans 12:17–21. How might confronting someone in sin allow you to better live out these commands? How might you be able to live out these same commands by staying silent?

6. You Can Make Changes to Lessen the Consequences

Hopefully, by using some combination of the techniques listed above, you can start a healthy, honest, and productive conversation that leads to spiritual growth for everyone involved.

Sadly, some people will continue to harm themselves or others, and there are times when you simply cannot continue to overlook the behavior.

In situations like these, the best course of action may be for you to find ways to remove yourself from the situation, or at least lessen the consequences.

For example, if your parents or in-laws consistently act in a way that is hurtful to you or your family, you can choose to limit the amount of time you spend around them. If your friend always drains your energy with her constant complaining and negativity, you can choose not to be friends anymore. And if your husband is mean, manipulative, or abusive, please get the help you need.

While the Bible does warn us that we may suffer *for the gospel*,[1] nowhere does the Bible command us to endure others' abuse for fear of standing up for ourselves and our families.[2]

It is perfectly appropriate and biblical to set boundaries with anyone who consistently behaves in ways that are harmful to you, your family, or your friends. In situations like these, please be sure to speak with a trusted friend, family member, pastor, or counselor to help you find the right course of action for you.

Dive Deeper into Scripture

→ Read 1 Corinthians 5:1–7. Did Paul judge this Christian caught in obvious sin? What did Paul recommend be done to him as a result? Why did Paul suggest this (vv. 5, 7)?

→ Read 2 Corinthians 7:8–11. What effect did Paul's previous letter (from the question above) have on the Corinthian church?

12

Cultivating a Faith-Filled Mindset

How can I follow God's will
faithfully when life is hard?

Despite all the successes God has given us as we've built Equipping Godly Women over the past several years, two years ago, I went through a period marked by doubt, fear, and insecurity.

I wondered, *What if I heard God wrong? What if He didn't actually call me to build this ministry and my friends only believe me because I've been so confident about it?*

I didn't have any particular reason to doubt my calling. Nothing was wrong. And yet I suddenly felt woefully inadequate and unprepared for what I had previously believed God was asking me to do.

And this is only one of many times I've struggled with doubt, fear, and insecurity throughout my life. In college, I went through a time when I didn't even want to believe in God, much less follow Him. Since then, I often feel like I'm questioning everything.

Are my meager efforts enough? What if I've completely missed the mark? Am I working hard enough? Or am I trying too hard? Most days, I have no idea.

Throughout this book, we've looked at a plethora of Bible verses, tips, and guidelines to help you figure out how God might be calling you to live out your faith today.

But **sometimes the problem isn't that we don't know *what* to do, but our doubt, fear, and insecurity hold us back from where we *already know* God is calling us.**

Have you ever gone through your own season of doubt, fear, comparison, or insecurity? Maybe you sense God asking you to take the next step, but you don't know how or what it will look like. Maybe you don't feel up to the task.

If so, you're certainly not alone. Throughout the Bible, we see countless examples of men and women who doubted God's call, who were too afraid to take action, and who felt woefully unprepared for what He was calling them to do. They faced persecution, hardships, and trials.

And yet, they pressed on—despite their doubts, fears, and insecurities—and God used them in incredible ways.

Friend, **don't fall for the lie that just because God calls you to do or be something, it will always be easy, comfortable, or convenient. It won't.**

Following God's will for your life can be incredibly fun and fulfilling, but it can also be challenging, inconvenient, risky, and even downright terrifying.

That's why, in this chapter, we're taking a look at a few well-known Bible characters who struggled with doubt, fear, and insecurity and how they overcame these obstacles. We'll also look at several practical ways we can overcome our own doubt, fear, and insecurity.

Dealing with Doubt

Long before Moses stood up to Pharaoh, led the Israelites through the Red Sea, and gave us the Ten Commandments, he was an insecure fugitive shepherd with a speech impediment.

Scripture tells us that when God appeared to Moses in a burning bush, "Moses hid his face, because he was afraid to look at God" (Ex. 3:6b). And when God told Moses that he would lead God's people out of slavery, "Moses said to God, 'Who am I that I should go to Pharaoh and bring the Israelites out of Egypt?'" (v. 11).

Moses wasn't being humble or reverent here. He genuinely did not believe he was up to the task. Even after God performed two miraculous signs and assured Moses that He would be with him, Moses still insisted, "Pardon your servant, Lord. Please send someone else" (4:13).

Do you ever struggle with doubting God's goodness, His power, or His plan for your life? Maybe you wonder if you heard God correctly, as I did. Maybe you doubt God could use you, as Moses did. Maybe you doubt God's goodness, faithfulness, or intentions.

Maybe, like many of us, you know God *can* do miracles but you're not fully convinced He'll come through for *you*.

If any of this sounds familiar, read Moses's story to see how God can use even an insecure, fearful shepherd to fulfill His great purposes. Then we'll look at three practical ways you can overcome doubt as well.

Dive Deeper into Scripture

→ Read Exodus 3–4. What reasons did Moses give for
why he couldn't possibly obey God? How did God
respond? Did Moses ultimately obey or disobey?
What happened as a result?

I. Focus on God's Power—Not Yours

During my time at Christian university, one chapel speaker shared an encouraging message I'll never forget: When you feel overwhelmed by the great need around you, and you feel insignificant, small, and unprepared, let God's infinite goodness, power, and majesty overwhelm you instead.

This is the same powerful advice we see God give Moses in the desert.

When Moses questioned, "Who am I?" God didn't give Moses an encouraging pep talk. He didn't say, "You've got this!" or "You're so smart, brave, and talented."

Instead, God promised, "I will be with you."[1]

You see, Moses's effectiveness never rested in *his own* ability. It rested in *God's*. And the same is true for us. On our own, we can do very little. But when we partner with God … He can do *anything*.

2. Remember God's Faithfulness

In *Relentless: The Unshakeable Presence of a God Who Never Leaves*, author Michele Cushatt encourages readers to collect twelve small mementos to commemorate the ways God has come through for them in the past.[2] This is another practice we see outlined in Scripture,[3] and it's still every bit as effective today.

Have you ever seen God come through in your life in a real and remarkable way? If so, how can you memorialize, remember, and cling to God's past faithfulness in the future?

For example, you might purchase a piece of jewelry, display a quote on your wall, collect photographs in a scrapbook, write down stories in a journal, or even get a tattoo.

What would help you remember God's faithfulness when you're tempted to doubt?

3. Find Support and Encouragement

It's easy to feel as though you're all alone or that God has forgotten about you when you're going through various struggles and hardships. Yet chances are, you aren't the only one who is struggling.

This is why it can be so helpful to reach out to others who are in a similar situation and ask them for help, encouragement, and advice.

Would you find it empowering to join a support group for cancer survivors, abuse survivors, or former addicts? Maybe you'd like to connect with other moms who have suffered miscarriages, lost their husbands or children, or are dealing with scary medical diagnoses.

Groups like these are out there—you just have to find them.

Sandy's Story

My ex-husband and I separated when our daughter was only six months old. Suddenly, I was a single mom, working part-time, and on government assistance so I could support my daughter. When she was two, I became a Christian.

During this time, I had serious doubts about how I could raise this child on my own and if I'd ever meet a man who would want me, especially since I already had a daughter.

Thankfully, God's promises and His plan are truly for our good. Five years later, I met a wonderful Christian man who not only took me but also my daughter as his own. Thirty years (and another child) later, we are still married, praising God and trusting Him for everything.

I do still have doubts from time to time about other things. I'm human. But it only takes seconds for me to remember who holds my future. Praise His holy name!

Dealing with Fear

If anyone had reason to fear, it was Daniel. When Babylonian King Nebuchadnezzar conquered Jerusalem, Daniel was captured as a prisoner of war and forced to join the king's service. Yet Daniel and his friends Shadrach, Meshach, and Abednego boldly resolved to follow God no matter the cost. It wasn't long before their faith was tested.

In Daniel 3, King Nebuchadnezzar fashions a large gold idol, approximately one hundred feet tall,[4] for the people to worship. The king's herald proclaims, "Whoever does not fall down and worship will immediately be thrown into a blazing furnace" (v. 6).

But Shadrach, Meshach, and Abednego know better than to worship a foreign idol. They refuse, and King Nebuchadnezzar throws them into the furnace, heated seven times hotter than normal. The fire is so hot that the king's own soldiers die, but miraculously, Shadrach, Meshach, and Abednego survive the flames unharmed.

Three chapters later, the king's men conspire to kill Daniel, who has gained a great deal of influence in the nation. They convince Darius, who is now ruling the kingdom, to pass a law that anyone who prays to any god other than the king for the next thirty days is to be thrown into the lions' den.

It's safe to assume Daniel had heard what happened to Shadrach, Meshach, and Abednego. He knew the king would carry out his decree. And yet, despite the promise of death, Daniel continues to pray three times every day anyway, just as he had done before. As a result, Daniel is thrown into the lions' den.

Sometimes our fears are small and unfounded. We might worry what others will think or what following God might mean for our future. Other times, following God can bring the threat of very real consequences.

Yes, there is a chance that following God could cost you your friends, your job, or even your life. But when we follow God in spite of these fears, we can trust that He will always come through in His time and His way.

On its own, fear isn't inherently sinful. It's a natural, normal response to change, growth, and uncertainty. However, we don't have to let fear run our lives. We can follow God in spite of our fear, trusting that He knows what He's doing and He will carry us through.

Read Daniel's inspiring story. Then we'll look at three ways you can push through fear and obey God, no matter the cost.

Dive Deeper into Scripture

→ Read Daniel 1, 3, and 6. How does Daniel and his friends' obedience in chapter 1 prepare them to stand up for their faith when the stakes become higher? How did God come through for these four men? How was God glorified as a result of these men's faithfulness? (Don't miss Daniel 6:25–27.)

1. Examine Your Fear

Fear can be an overwhelming, paralyzing, and powerful emotion. This is why it can be so helpful to pause and identify exactly what you're afraid of. It may not be what you think.

Are you worried your friends and family will criticize or reject you? Are you scared you'll lose your job? Are you terrified you'll fail (or succeed)? Are you worried you'll be embarrassed? What, specifically, are you afraid of?

Maybe you're scared you heard God wrong, or you're worried you might say or do the wrong thing and make a bad situation even worse. If so, you wouldn't be the first.

Jesus' own disciples messed up all the time. And God used them anyway. For example:

- The disciples frequently misunderstood Jesus' teachings (Matt. 16:5–12).
- They argued about who would be the greatest (Luke 9:46).

- They tried to stop a man from driving out demons (Luke 9:49).
- They rebuked parents for bringing their children to Jesus (Matt. 19:13–15).
- They were indignant when a woman poured perfume on Jesus (Matt. 26:6–13).
- Peter rebuked Jesus for talking about His death (Matt. 16:21–23).
- Peter cut off a servant's ear during Jesus' arrest (John 18:10–11).
- Peter also disowned Jesus three times before the rooster crowed (John 18:17, 25–27).

Thankfully, God doesn't expect us to follow Him perfectly. Even when we mess up, He can still use us in incredible ways.

Don't let a fear of getting it wrong keep you from pursuing God's best for your life. Instead, walk in faith, trusting that God will guide you as needed.

2. Evaluate Likely Outcomes

Once you've identified what exactly you're afraid of, it's often helpful to evaluate your beliefs to see if they're rooted in fact or fear.

For example, you may worry that your husband will leave you, your coworkers will exclude you, your friends will tease you, or your parents will be ashamed of you. But are these scenarios likely to happen, or are they just fears?

What is most likely to happen if you obey God's will for your life? What is likely to happen if you don't? And furthermore, even if your actions are uncomfortable at first, is there a chance they'll be worth it?

If you're following God's will for your life, the answer is yes.

3. Obey Anyway

And finally, if you're waiting until you aren't scared before you fully obey God, you might be waiting a long time. Fear doesn't magically disappear on its own, and it rarely diminishes with time.

This is why we must learn to obey God in spite of our fears rather than waiting for some imaginary day in the future when we'll never feel fear again.

I don't say this as someone who has this all figured out, of course. Even recently, I put off obeying God in one area of my life for *over a year* because I was too afraid of what might happen if I spoke up. And when I finally did obey, I learned my fears were mostly unfounded.

You may be familiar with the well-known quote, "Courage is not the absence of fear but rather the assessment that something else is more important than fear."

Sometimes the only way to move past fear is simply to push through, trusting that God will be with you every step of the way.

Dealing with Insecurity

While there's no question that our culture's social media obsession has fueled our desire and made it easier than ever before to compare ourselves to others, comparison—and the resulting insecurity that comes along with it—is really nothing new. We find a particularly painful story of comparison in the book of Genesis.

In Genesis 29, Jacob falls in love with Laban's daughter Rachel. Rather than giving Rachel to Jacob in marriage, however, Laban tricks Jacob into marrying Rachel's sister, Leah, instead. Not to be deterred, Jacob marries Rachel as well and works for seven more years to pay that debt to Laban.

Unfortunately for both of these women, Jacob doesn't even pretend to love his two sister-wives equally. Genesis 29:30a tells us, "Jacob made love to Rachel also, and his love for Rachel was greater than his love for Leah."

Even Scripture itself seems to favor Rachel over Leah. The first time we see these two women in Scripture, the Bible introduces them this way: "Leah had weak eyes, but Rachel had a lovely figure and was beautiful" (v. 17).

Have you ever compared yourself to someone else, only to come up lacking?

Maybe you feel a twinge of jealousy seeing all the other wives with their seemingly perfect, godly husbands, while yours refuses to step up. Maybe you feel like a total failure as a mom due to your children's out-of-control behavior. Maybe you've tried to set spiritual goals, financial goals, or health goals in the past, only to fail again and again.

Now, you read books like this and think, *That's great that those other women have found their calling. But that doesn't apply to me. I'm too [fill in the blank].*

Friend, Christianity isn't a competition. God doesn't line us all up at the pearly gates according to our weight, our charisma, or the number of good deeds we've done and let only the top ten thousand in. Where you are compared to other people really doesn't matter.

God created you exactly as *you* are to fulfill the unique role He wants you to fulfill. Do you have some room for improvement? Sure. We all do. (I know I do!)

Don't get so distracted focusing on all the ways you feel you don't measure up that you completely miss the unique role God created you to fulfill.

Here are three tips that will help you do just that.

Dive Deeper into Scripture

→ Read Genesis 29:13—30:24 and 37:1-11. Why is Leah jealous of Rachel in the first passage? Why is Rachel jealous of Leah? How does Jacob's and his wives' favoritism pass on to the next generation? (Note that Jacob was later renamed Israel.) Could this have been prevented?

→ Read Philippians 3:3-11. How was Paul uniquely qualified as a religious leader, preacher, and missionary? Why did Paul consider these impressive credentials "garbage"? Why do you think he felt this way? (Hint: See v. 9.)

I. Set Clear Goalposts

Follow too many people (especially influencers!) on social media, and it's easy to feel like everyone is good at everything … except you.

But this isn't the case at all. Everyone has different areas they excel at and struggle with, and a lot of what you see on social media is either fake or only showing part of the story.

This is why it's helpful to determine which goals actually matter to you (and which don't), as well as what level of "success" you'd personally like to see in each of these areas.

For example, I used to feel badly about myself when I saw other moms with perfectly decorated homes, who always had time for arts and crafts with their kids. Until eventually I realized: I don't actually want to be an arts-and-crafts type of mom! That isn't my goal. I simply felt like I *should* be because I saw other moms excelling in this area.

My goal as a Christian mom is to do my personal best to raise kids who love Jesus, who are smart and kind, and who know they can always come to me with any problem.

Once I got clear on my personal goals, I realized something: While my children and I rarely do arts and crafts together, we do spend a *lot* of time reading good books, snuggling on the couch together, and discussing all the ins and outs of Christianity—all activities that specifically support the type of mom I want to be, the type of relationship I want to have with my children, and the type of future I hope they grow into.

So what type of wife, mother, or Christian would you like to be?

Rather than pressuring yourself to measure up to everyone else's best, take some time to evaluate which goals actually matter to you. How much or how little do you want to excel in each area? And is pursuing these goals worth what it will cost you to get there?

Clearly identifying your own personal goals, standards, and expectations frees you up from striving to achieve someone else's perfect life and gives you the time and space to focus on your own.

2. Exchange Perception for Truth

We also have to keep in mind that what we see on social media isn't a true and accurate portrayal of everyone's life. It's only a carefully curated highlight reel.

Fitness influencers are rarely as thin as they look; they just know their best angles and filters. And parenting experts don't have perfect children; they simply highlight the fun, funny, or encouraging parts of motherhood, without sharing the rest.

Similarly, while I love to share tips on how to enjoy God's Word more consistently or how to live it out more authentically, this does not mean I always follow God's will perfectly myself. I have plenty of days when I don't feel like reading my Bible, and I have plenty of times when I struggle to obey.

We're all human. It's life. And it's a part of life that no one wants to share on Instagram.

This is why it's so important to take our friendships offline and connect in real life, where we can get to know people as normal, flawed, beautifully broken *people*, not as two-dimensional social media feeds.

Sara's Story

I struggle with comparison constantly. I see so many others who seem to have it "all together." Being a stay-at-home wife and mom is a lot, and I constantly feel like I don't do enough for my husband and daughters. I just have to remind myself that I will try my best and ask God to help me daily.

3. Reduce Temptation

If you regularly struggle with comparison, is there a pattern to your struggles? For example, is there one specific person or group of people who consistently make you jealous? Does reading certain magazines, books, websites, or social media accounts often leave you feeling "less than"?

If so, how can you find ways to reduce the temptations you face?

Personally, I am very careful about who I follow on social media, as I know that what I fill my mind with has the potential to dramatically affect my perspective. I don't want to fill my mind with the message that my looks, my home, or my parenting is all that matters. I don't want to waste my time feeling insecure, being jealous of someone else's success, or wondering why I'm not advancing quickly enough.

Instead, I choose to follow a smaller group of authentic people, businesses, and nonprofits who encourage and inspire me to be the best version of myself—not to measure up to their achievement. What might this look like for you?

Do you need to spend less time around people who cause you to feel insecure, unworthy, or "less than"? Do you need to delete social media off your phone, unsubscribe from certain magazines or websites, or be more careful about what you watch on TV? Do you need to befriend that woman who seems intimidating so you can see how normal she really is?

How can you prevent the temptation to compare before it happens?

Your Christian walk is too important to let it be derailed by doubts, fears, and insecurities.

Conclusion

Whenever my mom and I talk on the phone, after catching up on what's new in each of our lives, the conversation nearly always turns to Christianity. We may discuss what I'm working on at Equipping Godly Women, what we're reading in the Bible these days, or a question one of us has about how to live out God's Word in our day-to-day lives.

Recently, we were talking about this book and the topic of obeying God in general, when she commented, "You're the kind of person who sets her mind to something, makes a plan, and just does it."

I laughed. "Yes, with some things, but not everything. I definitely have my own struggles, doubts, and fears—the same as everybody else.

"But at some point—I don't remember exactly when—I finally committed to go *all in* with God and to obey Him no matter what," I explained.

"It isn't easy, and I definitely don't do it perfectly. I drag my feet a lot. But *every single time* I've obeyed God in the past, it has *always* worked out for my benefit. I have never regretted obeying anything God has asked me to do.

"I guess I've simply seen Him come through *so* many times now that *not* obeying doesn't even feel like a valid option anymore."

Friend, let me assure you, it was not always this way.

I still clearly remember being in high school, seeing youth leaders and other Christian women who seemed to have it all together, thinking there was no way I could ever be like that.

I had no idea how I could ever give up my sins, my fears, my failures, or my shortcomings. How I could give up control and obey whatever God asked of me. It felt so impossible. Like something "other" people did, that "normal" people could never aspire to.

But I'm here to tell you, that's not the case at all.

Yes, I run a Christian women's website, write books, and host conferences, but I can promise you that there is truly *nothing* that special or unique about me.

I'm still just a mom of three who struggles to trust, who yells at her kids too often, who looks like a mess most days, and who is selfish way more often than she cares to admit. Every single day, I feel like I'm failing at something (usually multiple somethings).

But somewhere along the way, I decided to trust that **God is who He says He is, He can do what He says He can do, and He knows what He's talking about**, even if I don't understand.

If God can use a scared fugitive (Moses), a shepherd boy turned adulterer (David), an unwed teenager (Mary), a religious fanatic and persecutor (Paul), and a ragtag group of men you'd never expect to be chosen (Jesus' disciples), He can certainly use me. And He can certainly use you.

Sure, it won't always be easy. You'll mess up, misunderstand, and drop the ball, and God may ask you to give up something you now hold dear.

But let me tell you: following God is always worth it.

So if you've ever looked at the amazing, incredible, inspiring Christian women all around you (either in person or online) and thought, *I want a faith like that*, the truth is, you can have it!

We all start somewhere. Why not start today?

Acknowledgments

When the team at David C Cook initially suggested a follow-up to *Fall in Love with God's Word*, I was immediately on board. Then the world shut down and things got crazy. This book truly would not exist without the help and hard work of a whole team of people who generously went above and beyond, each using their own unique God-given gifts to help get it across the finish line.

To my husband: If I listed all the things you do for our family, this book would be very long (and people would think I do nothing all day). Thank you for leading our family well, for saying yes to all my crazy dreams, for telling me gently when I'm wrong, for taking care of all the details I miss, and for somehow still thinking I'm cool enough to brag about to all your friends. I truly could not ask for a better husband.

To my children: Thank you for being so helpful, kind, and considerate while I worked on this book. Your dad and I are so proud of you, and I know God is too. I can't wait to see what amazing things God has in store for your futures as you continue to love Him and serve Him more than anything—just like you do now.

To my mom: You are, without a doubt, the godliest woman I know. Thank you for all the phone conversations and prayers and for setting an amazing example of what it means to be *all in* for God.

You've had a tremendous impact on this world—far more than you'll ever know.

To Stacey, Michael, and Stephanie: My first few attempts at this book were pretty awful. Thank you for the brainstorming calls, professional advice, and insightful feedback I needed to get unstuck. The end result is a book far better than I ever could have written on my own.

To Blythe, Susan, Judy, James, and Katie: Once again, you've been incredible to work with. I appreciate you and all your hard work!

To Jen, Alisyn, and Cassie: Thank you for your willingness to jump in and help out wherever needed. You have been a huge blessing, both to me and to our community at EGW.

To my readers at Equipping Godly Women: Thank you for so generously sharing your stories, your encouragement, and your questions. I hope you find this book helpful and encouraging to you as well.

And most important, to God: You and I both know what a disaster I am without You. Thank You for loving each of us at our worst and still promising us Your best (no matter how many times we blow it). Every good thing we have is all because of You, and I can't wait to see what You have in store next.

Notes

Chapter 1: The Two Greatest Commandments

1. "Matthew 22," Pulpit Commentary, Bible Hub, accessed August 1, 2021, https://biblehub.com/commentaries/pulpit/matthew/22.htm; "The Great Commandment (Matthew 22:34–40)," Gospel Light Christian Church, December 8, 2019, https://gospellight.sg/sermons/the-great-commandment-matthew-2234-40; "The Rules of the Pharisees," PursueGod.org, accessed August 1, 2021, www.pursuegod.org/rules-pharisees; Joseph M. Stowell, *Fan the Flame: Living Out Your First Love for Christ* (Chicago: Moody, 1986), 52, as paraphrased in "Pharisaic Laws," Bible.org, accessed August 21, 2021, https://bible.org/illustration/pharisaic-laws.

2. "The Rules of the Pharisees," www.pursuegod.org/rules-pharisees.

3. Jerry Bridges, "Jesus Challenges the Pharisees," Ligonier, May 17, 2008, www.ligonier.org/learn/articles/jesus-challenges-pharisees.

4. "The Rules of the Pharisees," www.pursuegod.org/rules-pharisees.

5. "Matthew 22:36," Pulpit Commentary, Bible Hub, accessed August 1, 2021, https://biblehub.com/commentaries/matthew/22-36.htm.

6. Matthew 21:12–13.

7. Mark 2:15–16.

Chapter 2: The Four Calls on Every Christian's Life

1. See also Mark 1:15.

2. *Merriam-Webster*, s.v. "repent," accessed March 8, 2022, www.merriam-webster.com/dictionary/repent.

3. Matthew 8:5–13.

4. Matthew 9:20–22.

5. Matthew 15:22–28.

6. "Rabbi and Talmidim," That the World May Know, accessed August 1, 2021, www.thattheworldmayknow.com/rabbi-and-talmidim.

7. "Rabbi and Talmidim," www.thattheworldmayknow.com/rabbi-and -talmidim.

8. "Being a First-Century Disciple," Bible.org, accessed August, 1, 2021, https://bible.org/article/being-first-century-disciple.

9. "The Stories They Tell—Voicemail from Flight 175," 9/11 Memorial & Museum, YouTube, accessed September 1, 2021, www.youtube.com/watch ?v=gulhkfAjTko.

10. "Rabbi and Talmidim," www.thattheworldmayknow.com/rabbi-and -talmidim.

Chapter 3: Understanding God's Written Word

1. 1 Corinthians 2:12.

2. This process has been adapted from J. Scott Duvall and J. Daniel Hays, *Grasping God's Word: A Hands-On Approach to Reading, Interpreting, and Applying the Bible*, 3rd ed.(Grand Rapids, MI: Zondervan, 2012), and Gordon D. Fee and Douglas Stuart, *How to Read the Bible for All Its Worth*, 4th ed. (Grand Rapids, MI: Zondervan, 2014).

3. 2 Peter 1:20–21.

4. James 1:5.

5. List adapted from Duvall and Hays, *Grasping God's Word*, 81.

6. Please see chapter 3 of my previous book, *Fall in Love with God's Word: Practical Strategies for Busy Women*, for more information about each of these biblical genres and how they affect our understanding of Scripture.

7. Duvall and Hays, *Grasping God's Word*, 45.

Chapter 4: Hearing God's Spoken Word

1. Genesis 37:5–10.

2. Exodus 3:1–4.

3. Numbers 22:21–31.

4. 1 Kings 19:11–13.

5. Acts 10:9–16; 16:9; 18:9–10.

6. Genesis 41:25.

7. Acts 10:9–16.

8. Romans 1:18–20.

9. Exodus 4:1–9.

10. 1 Samuel 3:4–5.

11. See Romans 8:1.

Chapter 5: Finding Opportunities to Serve

1. See Mark 6:1–6.

Chapter 6: Making Wise Decisions

1. Joel Hoomans, "35,000 Decisions: The Great Choices of Strategic Leaders," *The Leading Edge* (blog), Roberts Wesleyan College, March 20, 2015, https://go.roberts.edu/leadingedge/the-great-choices-of-strategic-leaders.

2. Genesis 3:6–7.

3. Exodus 32:1.

4. Deuteronomy 32:51–52.

5. Judges 16:18–21.

6. 2 Samuel 11:4, 15–17; 12:15, 19.

7. Acts 5:1–10.

8. Matthew 26:14–15; 27:3–5.

9. Luke 22:56–62.

10. Colossians 3:13.

11. Ephesians 5:33.

12. Matthew 22:39.

13. Proverbs 3:5.

14. 1 Thessalonians 5:22.

15. Michael Scanlan, *What Does God Want? A Practical Guide to Making Decisions* (Manchester, NH: Sophia Institute Press, 2018), 73.

16. Priscilla Shirer, *Fervent: A Woman's Battle Plan for Serious, Specific, and Strategic Prayer* (Nashville: B&H Publishing Group, 2015), 186.

Chapter 7: Cultivating Spiritual Disciplines

1. "Bible in One Year," Alpha International, 2022, www.bibleinoneyear.org.

2. While Catholics and Protestants pray slightly different variations of the Lord's Prayer (also called the Our Father), both come from Jesus' well-known prayer, recorded in Matthew 6:9–13 and Luke 11:2–4.

3. Officially known as the Gloria Patri, the Glory Be is a short prayer of praise to God, commonly said as part of the rosary as well as on its own.

4. Also known as the prayer of Mary or the song of Mary, the Magnificat is a traditional prayer based on Mary's words in Luke 1:46–55.

5. Elizabeth Manneh, "Lectio Divina: A Beginner's Guide," Busted Halo, March 1, 2021, https://bustedhalo.com/ministry-resources/lectio-divina-beginners-guide.

6. Luke 10:25–37.

Chapter 8: Standing Strong for What You Believe

1. Jim Rohn, Goodreads, accessed August 1, 2021, www.goodreads.com/quotes/1798-you-are-the-average-of-the-five-people-you-spend.

Chapter 9: Choosing Your Friendships Wisely

1. Brittany Ann, "Why Christians Belong in Bars," Equipping Godly Women, accessed July 24, 2021, https://equippinggodlywomen.com/community/why-christians-belong-in-bars.

2. The book *Boundaries* by Henry Cloud and John Townsend is a fantastic resource to help you determine what this might look like in your life.

Chapter 10: Witnessing with Truth and Love

1. "In U.S., Decline of Christianity Continues at Rapid Pace," Pew Research Center, October 17, 2019, www.pewforum.org/2019/10/17/in-u-s-decline-of-christianity-continues-at-rapid-pace.

2. David Kinnaman and Gabe Lyons, *unChristian: What a New Generation Really Thinks about Christianity … and Why It Matters* (Grand Rapids, MI: Baker Books, 2012), 72.

3. Kinnaman and Lyons, *unChristian*, 24–28.

4. John 16:33.

5. A few great books: *The Case for Christ* (Lee Strobel), *Cold-Case Christianity* (J. Warner Wallace), *Keeping Your Kids on God's Side* (Natasha Crain), *Mama Bear Apologetics* (Hillary Morgan Ferrer, Amy Davison).

Chapter 11: Speaking Up against Sin and Wrongdoing

1. 2 Timothy 1:8.

2. Again, the book *Boundaries* by Henry Cloud and John Townsend is a fantastic resource to help you determine what this might look like in your life.

Chapter 12: Cultivating a Faith-Filled Mindset

1. Exodus 3:11–12.

2. Michele Cushatt, *Relentless: The Unshakeable Presence of a God Who Never Leaves* (Grand Rapids, MI: Zondervan, 2019), 20.

3. Joshua 4:20–24.

4. "How Long Is a Cubit?," Ark Encounter, accessed August 1, 2021, https://arkencounter.com/noahs-ark/cubit.

Recommended Resources

While I found these resources to be helpful guides to their respective topics, this doesn't mean I endorse *all* of their teachings.

Fall in Love with God's Word: Practical Strategies for Busy Women
Brittany Ann. Colorado Springs: David C Cook, 2021.

Fall in Love with God's Word Workbook: Practical Strategies for Busy Women
Brittany Ann. Equipping Godly Women Ministries, 2021.

What Does God Want? A Practical Guide to Making Decisions
Michael Scanlan. Manchester, NH: Sophia Institute Press, 2018.

Not a Fan: Becoming a Completely Committed Follower of Jesus
Kyle Idleman. Grand Rapids, MI: Zondervan, 2016.

Grasping God's Word: A Hands-On Approach to Reading, Interpreting, and Applying the Bible
J. Scott Duvall and J. Daniel Hays. Grand Rapids, MI: Zondervan Academic, 2020.

How to Read the Bible for All Its Worth
Gordon D. Fee and Douglas Stuart. Grand Rapids, MI: Zondervan, 2014.

How to Read the Bible in Changing Times: Understanding and Applying God's Word Today
Mark L. Strauss. Grand Rapids, MI: Baker Books, 2011.

The Will of God: Understanding and Pursuing His Ultimate Plan for Your Life
Charles F. Stanley. New York: Howard Books, 2020.

Whisper: How to Hear the Voice of God
Mark Batterson. Colorado Springs: Multnomah, 2020.

Frequency: Tune In. Hear God.
Robert Morris. Nashville: W Publishing Group, 2016.

The 4 Wills of God: The Way He Directs Our Steps and Frees Us to Direct Our Own
Emerson Eggerichs. Nashville: B&H Publishing Group, 2018.

Thou Shall: Freedom to Strip Away the "Nots" and Discover What God Really Wants
Jamie Snyder. Colorado Springs: David C Cook, 2014.

Pigeon Religion: Holy Spirit, Is That You?: Discerning Spiritual Manipulation
R. T. Kendall. Lake Mary, FL: Charisma House, 2016.

unChristian: What a New Generation Really Thinks about Christianity … and Why It Matters
David Kinnaman and Gabe Lyons. Grand Rapids, MI: Baker Book House, 2012.

Counter Culture: Following Christ in an Anti-Christian Age
David Platt. Carol Stream, IL: Tyndale, 2017.

Living in a Gray World: A Christian Teen's Guide to Understanding Homosexuality
Preston M. Sprinkle. Grand Rapids, MI: Zondervan, 2016.

Talking Across the Divide: How to Communicate with People You Disagree with and Maybe Even Change the World
Justin Lee. New York: TarcherPerigee, 2018.

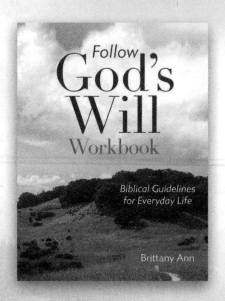